The Red Pear Garden

EDITED BY *John D. Mitchell*

INTRODUCTION BY *Richard E. Strassberg*

The
Red Pear
Garden THREE GREAT DRAMAS
OF REVOLUTIONARY CHINA

David R. Godine

DAVID R. GODINE PUBLISHER
BOSTON, MASSACHUSETTS

This book was published under the auspices of the
Institute for Advanced Studies in Theatre Arts.

Designed by Carol Shloss. Dustjacket and binding designed by Lance Hidy.

LCC 73-81068
ISBN 0-87923-073-8

To our friend Emanuel K. Schwartz, who touched each of us in turn and was the catalyst for this book.

FOREWORD

The Institute for Advanced Studies in Theatre Arts is deeply indebted to Bonnie R. Crown and Andrea Miller of the Asian Literature Program of The Asia Society for their encouragement and steadfastness as mentors for publication of *The Red Pear Garden*. As friend and colleague, Richard E. Strassberg was of great help and support in the planning of this anthology. The Institute also expresses gratitude to Roger Yeu of the Far East Asian Languages and Cultures Department of Columbia University for his enthusiasm and interest in a verse translation of *The White Snake* and his expert guidance on the musical aspects of Peking Opera. It extends thanks to Dr Daniel S. P. Yang, University of Hawaii, who tested the verse of *The White Snake* with the singing style and the traditional music of Peking Opera, providing insights for the poet William Packard. From its inception, Donald Chang, Peking-born and a teacher in the Far East Asian Languages and Cultures Department of Columbia University, shared his profound knowledge of the language of the original texts and the culture they reflect. His enthusiastic guidance proved essential.

The Institute wishes to express appreciation to the IASTA actors Peter Blaxill, George Gitto, Bella Jarrett, and Patricia Peardon; to the Peking Opera singing actors Jerome and Sophia Min; and to the Peking Opera musicians T. N. Chang, K. K. Choey, Delphine Sun, C. H. Pan, and S. Yeh. In the crucible of rehearsal and presentation of *The White Snake* they contributed invaluable insights that shaped the final verse translation. Thanks are also due to Gilbert Forman of the IASTA staff, who steadfastly saw the manuscript through the press.

J. D. M.

CONTENTS

INTRODUCTION
by Richard E. Strassberg

During the first half of the eighth century, China experienced a golden age under Tang Ming Hwang, the brilliant emperor of the Tang Dynasty.[1] The period was marked by a synthesis of excellence in many fields – literature, calligraphy, poetry, administration – one that was hard to equal in later times. Ming Hwang was an energetic patron of the arts, praised not only for his connoisseurship but for his creativity. The *Tang History* records that after holding court, he would have several hundred courtesans entertain him with a rudimentary form of drama.[2] They would generally present a story by singing and dancing to musical accompaniment. If there was a mistake in the music, the emperor would invariably notice and make corrections.

With Ming Hwang's great interest in training talent, high standards were maintained at the court. In 714, only a year after his enthronement, he established the Music Workshop (*Chyau Fang*) in the capital, Chang An.[3] Ming Hwang's interest in drama grew as his reign progressed, and entertainment began to occupy more and more of his time. Deciding that the Workshop was located too far away and maintained low standards, he organized a large corps of professional actors and courtesans under his personal patronage and instruction. They called themselves Students of the Emperor (*Hwang Di Dz Di*), and were located beside the Peng Lai Palace near the Imperial Park. They were not far from the famous Pear Garden and since they often performed there, they soon became known as Students of the Pear Garden (*Li Ywan Dz Di*). The wider theatrical world later became the Pear Garden Profession and, despite the changes of dynasties, the original identification with the Brilliant Emperor's court was remembered. The actors' awareness of the performing arts as entertainment and their personal relationships with an enlightened patron were cherished ideals of the traditional Pear Garden. Indeed, Tang Ming Hwang later became the patron god of the theatre, and prayers were offered to him before each performance.

Across a span of twelve centuries, the concept of the Pear Garden endured. As the art of drama increased in sophistication, new concerns and forms succeeded old ones. Yet as long as a distinct community of performers existed, detailed theatrical traditions continued to be passed down orally, professional pride was upheld, the entertainment value of theatre remained a prime concern, and the need for court or official patronage was felt. The history of the Red Pear Garden, that is, the Chinese theatrical world since 1949, is largely the alteration of the traditional Pear Garden under the recurrent pressure of Communist party authorities.

One of the fascinations of Communist China lies in the interplay between the demands of new ideology and the attachment to traditional cultural forms. China's cultural history often seems like a rolling handcar whose forward motion in time is due to the alternating pressures generated by these two forces. Yet the achievement of the larger goal of socialist reconstruction has not been consistent in all areas. By the time of the Liberation in 1949, the Communist party had achieved noticeable successes in the political and military spheres, which had little influence on the performing arts. Since 1949, the Red Pear Garden has been the scene of a struggle between activist ideas already consolidated in the ruling structure and permeating the society as a whole, and the inertia of traditional Peking Opera, rooted in a discredited society that still maintained some prestige. From one side comes the pressure of socialist theory and its demands on art. From the other comes the counterthrust of popular themes and a well-developed mode of presentation perfected during the centuries of Confucianism. Progress has been most erratic, often subject to the outcome of larger struggles in the political sphere. Since the Cultural Revolution, the state of theatre seems to be a victory for modern, revolutionary Peking Opera. The process whereby political forces were able to overcome resistance in the Red Pear Garden can best be understood by dividing China's recent cultural history into six important periods.[4]

1 THEORETICAL PREPARATION IN YENAN, 1942-1949 During these years, the Chinese Communist party had its headquarters in Yenan, in Northwest China. In the war against Japan (1937-1945) and the ensuing civil war against the Nationalists (1946-1949), the party was anxious to develop a 'Cultural Army' that would play a role in the larger struggle for control of China. To mobilize the cultural sector, conferences were held for party authorities to present guidelines for debate and implementation.

The ideological basis for a new kind of opera was stated at one
such conference by Mao Tse-tung in his 'Talks at the Yenan
Forum on Literature and Art' in May 1942.[5] This is an often-
cited article, and, with the recent canonization of Mao's thought,
it has become the ultimate pronouncement on the arts.

The 'Talks' are rooted in Lenin's view of the role of art in
the socialist state. All culture belongs to definite classes and
serves its class by presenting a particular political outlook. When
feudal classes hold power, art serves their interests and is a
weapon of control against the proletariat. In Communist China,
art must serve the workers, peasants, and soldiers by presenting
society through their eyes and showing the inevitable success of
the Revolution. Popularization is the prime artistic virtue. By
using the masses as a common denominator, art can reach its
audience and then attempt to uplift it. Aesthetic demands are
important to the extent that they make art a better tool. 'A thing
is good only if it brings real benefit to the masses.'[6]

During the Yenan period, organizations were set up to execute
socialist ideas in theatre. The Lu Syun Fine Arts Academy, the
Yenan Peking Opera Theatre and traveling peasant opera troupes
were vanguards in the cultural army. Old operas were performed
with minor revisions, historical operas written from a people's
viewpoint, and contemporary operas created using new dramatic
techniques. In the new operas, the themes emphasized were those
that could appeal to the downtrodden and unawakened proletariat. Resisting Japan, reducing rents, exposing traitors and supporting the Red Army, loving the people, and increasing production were frequent subjects.

The true state of the theatre in liberated areas nonetheless
remained overwhelmingly traditional, and new plays were ad-
mittedly limited propaganda efforts rather than a new art form
growing out of the society. This period is important not for its
actual successes in drama, which were few, but for its establishment of basic theoretical and practical approaches to the problem
of creating a socialist Chinese theatre. The conference as an
artistic forum, the organization of actors into institutions responsible to and funded by the authorities, and the ideological
direction of the Communist party were methods developed during this time. In later periods traditional forces continued to
struggle against these structures but the party inevitably cited

the principles of the Yenan period in pushing forward the revolution in opera.

2   With the Liberation in 1949, the party quickly consolidated its
SELECTIVE position on the mainland and pressed on to introduce pervasive
BANNING OF changes in Chinese life. It was a period of great pressure on tra-
OLD PLAYS, ditional society and the initial impulse to bend with the wind left
1950-1955 the old culture with few spokesmen.

The party used the techniques and guidelines developed during the Yenan period to deal with a flourishing traditional theatre. The initial organization was the national conference, held in Peking. These conferences gathered together for the first time representatives of the Red Pear Garden. Not only were traditional actors present, but modern playwrights, institutional personnel, and party cadres. Several keynote addresses, to be widely published after the conference, set forth the object. Minor addresses would be given, followed by discussion. After adjournment, the participants were expected to return to their localities and follow the guidelines set forth in the speeches. The Red Pear Garden was forced to accept the people's viewpoint: to regard theatre as a weapon of the Revolution and to incorporate Western stage techniques. At the same time that the traditional basis of the Pear Garden was being undermined, the party seemed to have stepped into the role of patron and teacher.

Standing committees were established under the Ministry of Culture. Their purpose was to permanently integrate the diverse members of the Red Pear Garden and place them under party leadership. The Standing Committee for Theatre Reform (*Syi Jyu Gai Ge Wei Ywan Hwei*) publishd a list of twenty-six forbidden plays in 1952. Among them was the popular *Hu Dye Meng* (*The Butterfly Dream*); it was on the forbidden list because of its feudalistic depiction of women. By 1956 it quietly returned to the repertory; popular audience demand seemed to prevail. The traditional theatre world, with it highly individualized and capitalist structure, was organized into theatre institutes, opera schools and troupes. All were to some extent state-supported and were responsible for carrying out the guidelines of the conferences.

Despite the impetus of the Revolution and the institutional support and the cooperation of key members of the Red Pear

Garden, the drive to reform opera started slowly, and the re-
siliency of traditional theatre became apparent. In terms of what
was being performed, reform was still very superficial. The
number of plays banned hardly touched the immense repertoire
of Peking Opera. Numerous traditional plays as objectionable as
those on the government list continued to be staged. The writing
of new operas was not progressing fast enough. Too few were
being performed too often. The troupes could not or were unwilling to learn the new pieces quickly and continued to play the
steady favorites.[7] The people themselves still preferred to see
stories of generals, prime ministers, scholars, and beauties. For
all their apparent acceptance of the image of the model Communist, the old ideals, it seems, were still entrenched.

The authorities were not beyond using pressure to enforce
compliance. Troupes were disbanded, costumes and properties
confiscated and individuals were punished as examples. Towards
the end of the period, discontent in the Red Pear Garden became
obvious, and discussions began about the precise relationship of
the authorities to the theatre organizations.

From June 1 to 15, 1956, a national conference was held in Peking to deal with all plays in the repertoire. The seventy-nine
members were the same cadres, artists, and writers who were now
the recognized representatives of the Red Pear Garden. As the
conference progressed, numerous opinions supporting traditional
opera were voiced. Those plays that demonstrated class struggle,
elevated the masses, and had artistic and entertainment value
should be performed with little change. Evaluation of old plays
should have limited objectives. The high-handed methods used
by cadres were criticized, and it was suggested that the role of
party authorities in setting artistic policy should be reduced. As
a result, many previously banned plays were staged once more
and the theory of theatre as entertainment became popular again.

In February 1957 Mao Tse-tung gave a speech that launched
the Hundred Flowers Movement. A second national conference
was called, which resulted in the lifting of all restrictions what-
soever. The initial ban, it was explained, had been to consolidate
the Revolution and overcome the low awareness of the people.
But now the masses could distinguish between 'fragrant flowers'
and 'poisonous weeds.' In fact, the playwright Tyan Han stated

3
THE RELAX-
ING OF RE-
STRICTIONS,
1956-1957

that bad plays were no more than one percent of the entire repertoire and that theatre truly grew out of the working class.[8]

The revival of old plays was immensely popular, and theatres were crowded. Nevertheless, well-known actors such as Mei Lan Fang and Cheng Yan Chyou who had close government relations, urged the Red Pear Garden to act with self-restraint. Ten years later, during the height of the Cultural Revolution, Maoists were to view this period as one of anarchy, during which the forces of feudalism counterattacked and regained lost ground. Many of those who advocated traditional opera were later to be denounced.

4   In the relaxation of controls during the preceding period, few
'WALKING   modern operas were written or performed. Yet there was great
ON BOTH   feeling in the party that Peking Opera was straggling behind the
FEET,'   general push towards socialist reconstruction. Cadres continued
1958-1962   to warn actors not to ignore modern operas, but the revival of interest did not come until the Great Leap Forward in 1958. In that year, the party's Central Committee set forth the General Line of Building Socialism in which opera was to be a primary weapon of propaganda.

The Ministry of Culture called a national conference in Peking to discuss how opera could present modern life. A revolution in the theatre was advocated as a way of creating unity with workers, peasants, and soldiers, but this was still to be accomplished through the traditional techniques essential to Peking Opera. The work of re-editing old operas was to go on. The popular slogan 'Walk on Both Feet' originally meant dual development of industry and agriculture, but in the Red Pear Garden it signified development of modern operas and preservation of traditional ones. More conferences were held and the conclusion was reached to increase production of modern operas to 50 percent of the entire repertoire. There was a frenzy of competition.[9]

If one were to judge the results of these efforts by again considering what was being performed, the conclusion would have to be that the second revolution in Peking Opera was far from successful. At the Tenth Anniversary of the People's Republic in 1959, of the seventeen plays performed in celebration, only one was a modern opera. Lists of plays performed by major troupes in 1960-1962 showed that only a handful of modern operas were actually being staged. The failure of the Great Leap Forward in the economic sphere seemed to be reflected in the continuing traditional repertoire of Peking Opera.

While China recovered economically from the Great Leap Forward, the memory of the abrupt departure of Soviet advisors remained strong. Tensions continued to develop within the party itself, and the demon of 'Modern Revisionism,' i.e., Soviet betrayal of Communism became a major ideological preoccupation. A party meeting was called in 1962 to oppose Modern Revisionism in all quarters and strengthen class education. Traditional culture was widely criticized as containing inevitable traces of the feudal outlook. Failure of art to reflect the contradictions and struggles of the present was noted, and another 'Revolutionize Peking Opera Movement' was launched.

5
THE GROWTH OF MODERN REVOLU- TIONARY PE- KING OPERA, 1963-1965

The following year the Ministry of Culture called a national conference under the auspices of the Chinese Opera Institute to discuss problems of form and content in expressing modern themes. Despite more than ten years of socialist progress, many feudal and reactionary tendencies remained in old operas. Though Peking Opera had the widest popularity of any performing art, it was criticized as most incompatible with the demands of the proletariat.

One of the most significant events in this period was the emergence of Chiang Ch'ing as an advocate of modern, revolutionary Peking Opera. Chiang was a former movie actress in Shanghai who made her way to Yenan during the 1930s, joined the Communist party, and married Mao Tse-tung. Little known during the intervening years, she reached her present political prominence through her energetic activities in theatre reform.

As early as 1962 and throughout the following year, Chiang began to frequent the Red Pear Garden and express her dissatisfaction with the theatre's cultural lag. She investigated over one thousand plays and took an active role in the revising of the repertoire. Traveling widely, she found plays produced in Shanghai and brought them to Peking to be rewritten as modern Peking Operas.[10]

Both Chiang and Mao decided to hold a meeting in 1964, at which thirty-five plays were presented, four under the personal leadership of Chiang Ch'ing. This was the first formal recognition of her position in cultural circles. Throughout 1963 and 1964, Mao made speeches criticizing artistic and literary circles for their feudal outlook and their failure to reflect the socialist revolutionary struggle. A succession of meetings were held all over the country. Momentum continued into 1965.

6
TRIUMPH OF
MODERN
REVOLUTION-
ARY PEKING
OPERA

In the midst of the growing criticism and revaluation, an article by Yau Wen Ywan entitled 'On the New Historical Drama *Hai Rwei's Dismissal*' appeared in the November 11, 1965 issue of the Shanghai *Wen Hwei Bau*. Properly regarded as the first shot of the Great Cultural Revolution, the article attacked the Peking Opera written by Wu Han in 1961. *Hai Rwei's Dismissal* is a historical drama dealing with an actual official of the Ming Dynasty (1368-1644) who confronted the exploiting gentry at the risk of his own career. Hai Rwei (1515-1587) is portrayed as determined to execute the guilty son of a former prime minister and, despite his dismissal, is able to do so. The dominant themes of the play are the return of the land to its rightful owners and the opposition of honest officials to tyrants. Yau's article bitterly attacked the use of historical analogy to satirize present personalities and events, the dependence on an individual official as savior instead of the masses, and the dilution of the real class struggle with notions of class harmony.[11]

The significance of this attack only becomes apparent in the light of the political tensions that had been straining the leadership for some time. Ever since the Great Leap Forward, and perhaps as early as 1956, there had been division over basic policy at the highest levels, and it had become clear to many that Mao Tse-tung had lost significant control over the party apparatus. This was equally apparent in the army when Peng De Hwai, then Minister of Defense, and Mao had a famous confrontation in 1959. A wide range of differences came up, ranging from criticism of the Great Leap, relations with the Soviet Union, modernization of the army with nuclear weapons, and even Mao's continued leadership. Mao was able to mount a counterattack that ended in the dismissal of Peng and his supporters. But Peng's criticism had considerable support, and Mao's opponents ranged from Liu Shao-ch'i, then president and Mao's successor, down through the army, the party, and the bureaucracy. *Hai Rwei's Dismissal* is supposed to be a veiled analogy to Peng as the loyal, dissenting official.

In the course of the Cultural Revolution, Mao operated from his base in Shanghai and brought about a thorough purge in every organization and aspect of Chinese life. Using his thought as ideological gunpowder, his followers championed a rigid Communist orthodoxy and a final renunciation of traditional culture against Revisionism. The Cultural Revolution produced widespread convulsions in the Red Pear Garden. Theatrical institutes and schools of opera were closed down and many more troupes were disbanded. Traditional actors were humiliated, forbidden to perform and often sent to the countryside to be re-educated. Writers were forced to recant and disavow all their previous work as feudal and reactionary. Many had to defend themselves on ideological charges and little has been heard of since from those who were once prominent. In this most recent period a whole section of the cultural picture is said to have been erased and one wonders to what extent the Red Pear Garden is still recognizable. Emphasis is on proletarian identity and political consciousness – on common bonds with the masses. Mandatory labor, in factories or fields, tends to blend individual roles and leaves little time for the arduous training formerly required. Traditions that are neither developed nor passed on are bound to wither away.

Perhaps most important is the diminishing interaction between traditional culture and socialist ideology. By banning all but revolutionary operas from the stage, and by uprooting that part of the Pear Garden where traditional theatre still flourished, a major force in contemporary China's cultural progress has been neutralized and dispersed. If the victory of ideology over tradition is as complete as mainland sources would have us believe, there must be the eerie feeling of an empty battlefield. The old pressure forward momentarily subsides until new forces become apparent and realign themselves. As the country continues to develop independently under Mao Tse-tung's thought, the new society will produce a theatre that will be only related indirectly to the old heritage. With the recent end of the Cultural Revolution, the struggle will shift to one between forces within socialist culture. But if China's renewed interest in the outside world is more than diplomatic, it may well be the Western theatre that offers new viewpoints. Modern, revolutionary Peking Opera can be seen as a turning point in the development of Chinese theatre. If anything, it indicates that the Pear Garden is thoroughly Red.

This anthology presents three selections from the Red Pear Garden – all Peking Operas written since 1949.

The Institute for Advanced Studies in the Theatre Arts commissioned these translations and adaptations in the hope that they would be performed by American professional actors. For a practical theatre text, the decision was reached to use a system of romanization that would enable actors with no knowledge of the Chinese original to speak the character names and place names, so that they would approximate the sounds spoken by native Chinese. Since World War II the Yale University system of romanization has been widely taught; it is the conviction of the writers that this system meets the practical needs of actors and will best serve the reader interested in Chinese theatre.

Two of the operas are directly rooted in the traditional theatre and the third, though revolutionary, has interesting connections with the past. In the separate discussions below, only a few aspects have been singled out to emphasize the interaction between tradition and ideology. In analyzing actual plays, it can be seen that tradition is a powerful force that makes itself felt in various forms. The use of a long-established theme, the evocation of an entire world in the past and the duration of old mannerisms and patterns of behavior in the present enliven a whole range of traditional cultural values. Yet ideology is an equally strong force in its ability to alter the details of legends, reinterpret the entire past in modern terms, and, of course, create its own contemporary world where it is firmly in control. It is the balancing of these forces that is responsible for the greatest creativity in recent Peking Opera.

THE WHITE SNAKE

Throughout the history of Chinese fiction and drama, certain persistent themes have been treated again and again. Each time, themes have been altered – because of the demands of the different genres, the accretion of other themes, and progressive changes in the meaning of the story itself. These themes have been found to be most adaptable to such changes, and their endurance in the Red Pear Garden indicates the resilience of traditional culture.

The legend of the White Snake is thought to go as far back as the Tang Dynasty (618-907). As one of the most persistent of themes, it has been embodied in more versions than any other spirit-tale.

One of the earliest forms is a *Tsz Hwa* in the *Ching Ping Shan Tang Hwa Ben* collection.[12] The story, called *The Three Pagodas of West Lake* is set in the *Shwei Syi* era (1174-1189) of the Southern Sung Dynasty and is believed to have been written about that time. The hero, Syi Sywan Dzan, rescues the White Maiden, who has lost her way. He meets her mother, the Spirit in White and her grandmother, the Spirit in Black. Syi lives with the Spirit in White for half a year until she decides to kill him. He is saved by the White Maiden, however, and later, a Taoist priest captures all three spirits. The priest imprisons them under the three stone lanterns, well-known landmarks in West Lake. It is revealed that the White Maiden is a chicken spirit, the Spirit in Black is an otter spirit and the Spirit in White is a white snake.

In this rudimentary version, the White Snake appears as a demon who plagues men to willfully satisfy her own desires. She is a highly dangerous creature and lacks any redeeming human virtues. There is no doubt that the Taoist priest uses his superior magical powers for good and performs a service to mankind when he captures her. This early version also establishes the setting of West Lake in Hangchou, the capital of the Southern Sung and one of the most beautiful cities in China.

The mature version of the story dates from the late Ming Dynasty (1368-1644) when the author and editor Feng Meng Lung included it as Chapter 28 in his anthology, *Stories to Startle the World* (ca. 1620). The tale, written in imitation of the Sung storytellers, contains most of the elements familiar to later Chinese readers.

The hero, now named Syu Syan, meets Lady White and her sister Blue in a rainstorm at West Lake, sometime during the *Shau Sying* period (1131-1162) of the Southern Sung Dynasty. By borrowing an umbrella, White insures their meeting again.

Syu returns, they are betrothed, and White gives him money to arrange the wedding. The money is found to have been stolen from an official treasury. Syu is discovered and put on trial. Though White is able to produce the rest of the money under mysterious circumstances, Syu is still exiled to Sou Jou. White manages to follow him there and explain that the sum was left her by her former husband and that she was innocent. Syu relents, they marry, and live happily. Yet he is never quite sure that she isn't a spirit. He meets a Taoist priest who gives him charms to use against his wife. White is aware of this, though, and when the charms prove useless, she confronts the priest. After a duel of magical powers, she overcomes him.

One day, when Syu is going to visit a neighboring temple, White decides to outfit him properly and gives him some new clothes. The clothes are found to be part of a recently stolen shipment of goods from a local pawnshop. Syu is again arrested and put on trial. Though White once more manages to have the rest of the goods returned, Syu is exiled to Jen Jyang. White finds him there and offers the same explanation – that the clothes belonged to her former husband. Syu accepts this and they reconcile once again. Syn decides to visit the Jin Shan Temple where the abbot, Fa Hai, notices him. Meanwhile White and Blue have sped through the rough waters of the Yangtze River to fetch Syu. When they reach the temple, Fa Hai confronts them as demons and they disappear under the water.

Syu now recognizes them as spirits and begs Fa Hai for help. Fa Hai urges him to return to Hangchow (which he can do as a result of an imperial amnesty), and they will all meet there again. Syu returns but finds that White has preceded him. A snake catcher is summoned to trap White but winds up fleeing in fear when she turns into a tremendous white snake. Syu is about to kill himself in despair when Fa Hai reappears. He gives Syu his alms bowl which Syu uses to trap White while Fa Hai captures Blue with incantations. Both are placed at Thunder Peak Monastery where, as legend has it, Syu raised the money for the famous pagoda built there.

The plot has been made considerably more complex in the later version. White remains a snake spirit who has defied heavenly laws (Buddhist and Taoist elements are mixed) to come down to earth and experience human love. Yet the later story exploits tendencies in her character that lean towards a real humanity. She may endanger Syu by her random thefts yet each time she appeals to his love for her and reminds him of the happiness they enjoyed together. However, the cruel side of her personality is not entirely eliminated. When Syu returns to Hangchow after his exile, she threatens to destroy the city and its people unless he returns to her.

Syu remains a weak character as his infatuation with White continues to overcome his inner doubts about her real identity. His passions cool, though, as he becomes possessed by fear and helplessness. Fai Hai, in the role of the priest, still remains a savior. He acts, not out of cruelty, but in obedience to a higher law – that each being must be true to his own nature. White's crime was that she overstepped her spirit nature. Though the latter version no longer suggests that she is motivated to deliberately torment men, her very desire to enjoy earthly pleasures is what produces distorting effects in the world of man.

Parallel to the tale's development in fiction was its treatment in drama and the performing arts. While vernacular fiction had, by the Ming period, developed separately from the storyteller's art, the legend retained its popularity in oral literature. Mention is made of *The White Snake* as a *Tau Jen*[13] song sung to the lute and as the first recorded *Tan Dz* sung to the three-stringed guitar.

The earliest extant drama is a *Jwan Chi* play in thirty-two acts by Hwang Tu Bi, written in 1738. Entitled *Thunder Peak Pagoda*, it employs the Buddhist notion of karma as the underlying basis for the action in the story. Syu was a mendicant priest in his former existence, and both he and White had committed deeds that had to be atoned for in his life. In the first act, Buddha enters and explains all this to the audience. Fa Hai thus becomes a messenger of the True Path and he works for the salvation of both. Though the play was later revised and expanded to thirty-eight acts, it was still criticized for its style and lack of theatrical appeal.

Thirty years later, Fang Cheng Pei rewrote the story as *The Standard Version of Thunder Peak Pagoda* (1768). He was apparently unaware of the Hwang version and compiled his play from actor's scripts. The play gained in dramatic technique. More dialogue was added and there is less technical virtuousity in the poetic arias. Blue's role is expanded to the point where she is an active element in the relationship between Syu and White, becoming appropriately suggestive when White's shyness stands in the way.

The Hwang version follows the Ming story closely for White does not reveal herself to her husband as a white snake. In the Fang version, the act 'Dragon Boat Festival' has been added. Syu persuades White to get drunk in celebration and she does so because her love for him overwhelms her judgment. After drinking the wine, she reverts to her original form and Syu faints in shock. This heightens the tension between the two. Together with the two incidents of stolen money and goods, Syu is given reason to break with White. The play continues the historical process of humanizing White's character. Her intense yearning for earthly love is seen to be her only motive and the attachment between the two is shown to be more intimate. Her virago temperament is softened and in her conflicts with spiritual authorities, she shows the determination of a woman fighting to save her marriage.

The play adds to the legend by arranging for White to become pregnant and give birth to a son. Her ties to the human world are strengthened as she prepares to fulfill the additional role of mother. Her pregnancy allows her to spend a few more months with Syu in Hangchow where her happiness is most complete. Nevertheless, her spirit nature cannot be denied and she must be imprisoned by Fa Hai under the pagoda as punishment. Because the play has elements of Buddhist thought, no one can be denied salvation for long. In the final acts, White's release is ordered by the emperor and she is conducted to Paradise.

This version completes the traditional tale of the White Snake. The tragedy of the main characters lies in their inability to transcend their own roles and realize their personal desires. Syu, as a man, can never be at ease with a snake spirit; White, despite her yearnings, can never truly become human. Buddha's law remains inexorable, though not without its final mercy. For traditional Chinese, these facts were comfortably accepted. In their theatre, they did not look for plot solutions at the expense of the social and cosmological order.

The White Snake legend developed over a period of a thousand years. With the Liberation in 1949 and the subsequent call to rewrite traditional plays, *The White Snake* was again treated in a Peking Opera by Tyan Han. He started it during World War II and worked on it for about thirteen years, until it satisfied him.

Tyan has created a version of the White Snake legend that takes its place in the long tradition of Chinese fiction and drama and yet, by its revolutionary socialist outlook, has made significant alterations in the traditional plot, characterization, and theme. Gone is the role of the Buddha, the emperor, or any traditional authority figure who acts as a final appeal. The hero, renamed Syu Syan, is no longer a vacillating mortal victimized by his passions and unable to deal with spiritual beings. Tyan develops him into a loving, devoted husband with intense sympathy for White. White herself loses all fearsome qualities, and symbolizes warmth, intelligence, bravery, and chastity. Far from intending to harm him, she goes to great lengths to procure the sacred mushrooms and save his life. The two scenes where her thefts cause his exile are eliminated.

A radical change takes place in the character of Fa Hai, who becomes the villain. Though superficially a priest who has abandoned worldly concerns, he is depicted as an instrument of feudal forces working against the people. When the relationship of Syu and White was seen as contrary to heavenly law, Fa Hai was a correcting, merciful influence. Tyan, however, has emphasized White's search for love as a legitimate striving for freedom. Fa Hai acts now only as an obstruction, ignorant and malicious.

It is common for critics to see the play's conflict in terms of Maoist contradictions. There are the inner contradictions within White when her spirit nature interferes with her human desires. The contradictions between White and Syu reach their height in Scene Five, 'The Wine Incident,' when she turns into a white snake. Finally, there are the contradictions between White and Fa Hai. Contradictions are resolved by struggle. Personal conflict is seen as the only solution, mirroring the larger struggle of social forces. This reaches a climax in Scene Twelve, 'The Water Battle.' In the traditional versions, White and Blue are forced to dive beneath the river and escape when Fa Hai reveals they are demons. Now, however, Tyan Han has White rally the water creatures and attack Fa Hai's temple in a fashion reminiscent of the storming of the Winter Palace during the Russian Revolution. In Scene Sixteen, 'The Falling of the Tower,' White is freed, not through the intervention of any higher authority, but by the struggle of Blue's mass army with that of the Tower God.

The White Snake legend can be reinterpreted as an allegory of the historic struggle of the Chinese people against feudal oppression. This seems to be Tyan's viewpoint. White's personal search for love has wider implications, just as in her struggles she receives 'mass' support. The play was well received in China when it was published, but since the Cultural Revolution, it seems to have suffered the common fate of most interpretations of traditional culture. Indeed, with the present outlook restricted to modern, revolutionary Peking Opera, Tyan Han's version may well represent the final embodiment of the legend of the White Snake.

In this translation, the strict rhyme sequence of the Chinese text has been retained. Whenever a Chinese rhyme occurs, an English equivalent has been used, although in some cases, there may be only a single instance of the rhyme word and so it will not 'rhyme' in the Western sense of repetition. The key Chinese rhymes of *an*, *au*, and *ang* dominate *The White Snake* and William Packard chose the English equivalents respectively of *e*, *e*, and *and*. Some of these key rhymes recur as often as thirty times in a row and the task of finding the most adequate English rhymes was most difficult. At best, these sections achieve a curious fusion of rhyme that is rarely attempted in the West.

The syllable convention of the Chinese text has also been strictly followed. Some lines are only four syllables long and these must be miracles of compression. Most lines are between six and ten syllables in length, although there are occasional lines of eleven, twelve, thirteen, or even sixteen and seventeen syllables.

To retain the purity and simplicity of the original, the adaptor has tried to keep the tone of the diction in English as elemental and straightforward as possible. He has tried to use mostly simple monosyllables and avoid latinate forms, hyphenations, and contractions whenever possible.

Three distinct types of speech occur in the opera. In this adaptation, the 'dialogue' is written in free verse, with no syllable or rhyme requirements. The 'recitatives,' which are spoken but not sung, are indicated by syllable requirements on the right hand margin, as well as rhyme requirements. The 'arias' also have both syllable and rhyme requirements listed on the right hand margin.

This translation of *The White Snake* is based on the 1955 *Dzwo Jya Chyu Ban She* edition published in Peking. With American professional actors, Chinese singers, and Chinese musicians, *White Snake* was performed under the joint auspices of the Asia Literature Program of the Asia Society and the Institute for Advanced Studies in the Theatre Arts (IASTA) at Asia House, 1972.

THE WILD BOAR FOREST

In the revaluation of culture that followed the Liberation, few books were as enthusiastically embraced by Chinese critics as *Shwei Hu Jwan*.[14] The novel was seen as a vivid description of an actual peasant revolt led by Sung Jyang against the Northern Sung Dynasty (960-1127) in the year 1121. The first half of the one hundred and twenty chapters tells of the gathering of the one hundred and eight heroes on Mt. Lyang. Each of them has found it impossible to live in a society where corruption and injustice abound. They form a heroic community dedicated to the concept of *yi*. Ethically, *yi* denotes righteousness and justice. On a personal level, it means friendship and recognition of the bond between heroes (never between man and wife, or between blood relations). Against them are arrayed the forces of a weak and insensitive government that views them as rebels and is determined to disperse them. Despite the many campaigns against Mt. Lyang, the government armies are unable to defeat them. The second half of the novel relates the group's decision to declare their loyalty to the emperor despite his corrupt officials. The emperor's court uses the band to suppress other bandits and, in the later chapters, we see the final demise of the heroes through trickery and the attrition of battle.

Sung Jyang's revolt at Mt. Lyang is a historical fact. Critics were delighted to find an incident that confirmed the Marxist view of Chinese history as a succession of class struggles. Yet the historical evidence on the revolt is extremely meager. *Shwei Hu Jwan* as a novel is in no way an accurate account of the revolt or its individual participants. The book itself was derived from a popular cycle narrated by storytellers during the Southern Sung Dynasty (1127-1279). Whether it was due to nostalgia for the fallen Northern Sung, the attraction of the heroic personality, or popular sympathy for the outlaws, the narrative cycle became one of the most enduring in Chinese literature. The edition of one hundred and twenty chapters was published early in the seventeenth century, and an abbreviated seventy chapter version appeared about the same time.[15] Authorship of the novel is ascribed to Shr Nai An (1290-1365) and his disciple Luo Gwan Jung (1330-1400).

As literature, however, the novel has been criticized for wavering between nonhistorical mythmaking and the desire to present the story as fictionalized history.[16] The heroic personality is brought out in incidents that are clearly the product of the storyteller's imagination. The heroes are capable of superhuman feats of strength. Whereas the revolt in 1121 was no doubt based on economic and political factors, few of the heroes are shown in the novel to be motivated by any degree of social consciousness. Their gathering together on Mt. Lyang is due less to the common social conviction that history supposes than to their own violent natures. There is a problem for those who wish to see the novel as a record of true events emphasizing a consistent political ideology.

The Wild Boar Forest is based on Chapters 7-9 of the edition of *Shwei Hu Jwan*. Of all the incidents in the book, socialist critics have hailed this as the most successful for it presents the central character, Lin Chung, as an innocent man forced by an oppressive government to flee to Mt. Lyang.

Lin Chung, though not a peasant, represents the petty bourgeoisie beset by illusions. As a captain in the Imperial Guards, he has identified himself with the Establishment and looks forward to receiving its promotions and benefits. In time, he hopes to rise through the ranks and join the ruling class. This gives his character its dual nature. On the one hand, he is a courageous military man of goodwill, holding *yi* above all. But he appears weak before his superiors and suffers insults and injustice in order to save his position. Such restraints prevents him from completely dedicating himself to *yi* and are damaging to his reputation. As a member of a lower, oppressed class, he can never feel liberated until he manifests his hatred and gains vengeance.

The Wild Boar Forest relates the gradual development of Lin Chung's political consciousness and the release of his hatred for his oppressors. When Gau Shr De makes advances to his wife, Lin Chung is restrained, hoping the whole matter will blow over and his position will be saved. Gau represents the venality of the ruling class and he is determined to acquire Lady Jang at all costs. Only in the eighth scene when Lin realizes that his former classmate Lu Chyan is helping Gau plot against him does he begin to see that he is no longer safe. In Maoist terms, he begins to realize the contradictions inherent in his position. In the play, the primary contradiction is between Lin and Minister Gau and his son. As the plot progresses, Lin confronts their underdogs Lu Chyan, Fu An, and the two guards Dung Ping and Sywe Ba.

After the initial aggression by Gau Shr De and the ruse of the sword, Lin Chung is confronted by the two guards who are ordered to kill him. Though saved by the monk Lu Jr Shen and advised to return and gain revenge, Lin still insists on sparing the guards and going into exile. Such restraint is rare among the heroes of Mt. Lyang. The climax of the play comes after Lu Chyan follows him to Tsang Jou and burns the granaries. This, together with the news that his wife has committed suicide makes Lin realize that there is no way that he can make peace with his enemies. Unleashing his fury, he brings down a final vengeance on them and clarifies his position in the world. The play ends with Lu Jr Shen and Lin rejoicing over the bloody scene. In the novel, Lin proceeds to Mt. Lyang and becomes one of its one hundred and eight heroes. The audience realizes this, and sees *The Wild Boar Forest* as the awakening of a hero who will then go on to settle the score with Minister Gau.

In addition to its political theme of liberation and struggle, the play's popularity was due to its presentation of the traditional heroic personality. Both Lu Jr Shen and Lin Chung are among the most famous of the heroes who assemble on Mt. Lyang. Lu exemplifies 'animal exuberance.' He is a ferocious monk who eats meat, drinks wine, and uses his stick to battle anyone who offends him.[17] In the third scene, he demonstrates the hero's prerequisite of immense strength and skill by dealing with a group of ruffians who come to steal. Later, he uproots a tree with ease.

Equally important is the recognition given and received by heroes, and the ruffians at once recognize Lu's superior qualities. Unable to defeat him, they capitulate and declare themselves his followers. When Lin Chung sees Lu exercising in the garden he, too, recognizes his heroic nature. Naturally, members of the heroic community can identify each other and the two swear brotherhood.

Throughout the play, Lu is a free agent, befitting his heroic role. He roams the countryside correcting injustice and coming to the aid of his 'brothers.' Lu is aware of the danger involved when a hero, with his uncompromising sense of *yi*, is caught in a situation where he must deal with petty men who are his superiors. After the incident at the temple, he advises Lin to get out and 'avoid other people's breath.' It takes his wife's death to make Lin realize that he no longer has a stake in society. Only then can he give himself over completely to the heroic vision.

The Wild Boar Forest, as it was performed by the Peking Opera Troupe in China and also on tour in Europe and Canada, represents a traditional Peking Opera that has undergone a minimum of re-editing. It was possible to accept the world of Mt. Lyang and the viewpoint of the heroes as revolutionary and proletarian. The dedication to *yi* was a demand for social justice. The methods employed emphasized the contemporary virtues of bravery, loyalty, and unity. The heroes had an appealing moral authority, for what started as a small group grew rapidly as people fled to Mt. Lyang from great distances. *Shwei Hu* represents the archetypal world of resistance in China and presents a pattern of action later followed by many groups. Wartime Yenan was not unlike Mt. Lyang in its remote location and defiant spirit. As that era of Communist history recedes from memory, it is presented more mythically, and the parallels seem to grow. If there was anything in traditional culture that could reinforce the present it was the story of the heroes of Mt. Lyang.

Yet even *Shwei Hu* was not immune to the fierce attack on the past that was part of the Cultural Revolution. The extreme vanity of its heroes could not be defended; nor could their cruel and often senseless attacks against neutral peasants, or their lack of a comprehensive program of revolution. The final betrayal and destruction of the band was inexcusable and the heroes were blamed for their lack of insight towards the emperor and the exploiting official class. Had the criticism occurred during a more moderate period, changes in the legend could have been made. Coming as it did during the Cultural Revolution, the only course was a complete disavowal of the world of *Shwei Hu* and the ideal of the traditional hero.

The translation used here is based on the performance script of *The Wild Boar Forest*. The Chinese text has been printed on the dust-jacket of the recording made by the National Troupe of Peking. The play was performed by the Peking Troupe on its international tour in 1960. One of the translators, John D. Mitchell, watched the performance in Montreal. The staging was traditional, performed as it would have been on a typical Peking teahouse stage of the nineteenth century. Under the influence of the Western stage, however, the act curtains of the proscenium theatre were used and elements of scenery and nontraditional properties were introduced.

TAKING TIGER MOUNTAIN BY STRATEGY

The modern revolutionary Peking Opera, *Taking Tiger Mountain by Strategy*, has been described by its authors as a play of struggle. The struggle was not only internal, with its theme of Liberation, but external, for the play itself emerged only after numerous conflicts with its 'enemies.' First written and performed in 1959, it is said to have reached prominence only when Chiang Ch'ing emerged as a cultural commissar. It was she who discovered the play in 1963 in Shanghai and guided it to its final form despite the 'wrecking activities' of Lyou Shau Chi and his followers.[18]

The countryside setting of the play and the ideological keynote of Mao Tse-tung's instructions to 'establish Firm Bases in the Northeast' (Scene One) seem to revive an old party struggle of the 1940s.[19] Peng Jen, head of the Municipal Party Committee of Peking, who was deposed during the Cultural Revolution, is said to have once opposed Mao's strategy of 'leaving the high road alone and seizing the land on both sides.' He evidently favored peace negotiations with the fortified cities of the Nationalists. The struggle of the play to preserve this theme against those who have made significant changes is seen as parallel to the greater political struggle of the Cultural Revolution, during which Mao rooted out the Revisionist clique of Lyou, Peng, and others.

In the play itself, certain principles were established to create a synthesis of revolutionary realism and revolutionary romanticism; something 'nearer the ideal and thus more universal than everyday life.' The main emphasis has shifted away from plot towards characterization of class heroes and enemies. The greatest criticism of traditional drama was that it was under the domination of elite classes and portrayed the people 'as though they were dirt.' With the victory of socialism in 1949 and the somewhat later canonization of Mao Tse-tung's thought, the goal of all revolutionary drama became the elevation of the proletariat on the stage. Each character embodies the motivations of his class, and the success of Yang Dz Rung, Di Yung Chi, and Shau Jyan Pwo over Mountain Vulture is the triumph of a unified proletariat against its feudal enemies.

Yang Dz Rung's 'banditlike airs' in the original were criticized as demeaning. In an early version he sang obscene ditties on his way up to Tiger Mountain, he flirted with Mountain Vulture's daughter, Rose, and told ribald stories in the bandits' stronghold. This earthy aspect was deleted and his heroic role as a class hero was reinforced. The third scene, 'Bitterness in the Mountains,' was added to show his sympathy with the masses and their instinctive warmth towards him. He has little difficulty overcoming Hunter Chang's doubts and he becomes the agent for Chang's emotional conversion to the Communist party.

Yang is fully armed with the words of Mao Tse-tung. Instead of singing obscene ditties, the arias he performs on the way up Tiger Mountain suggest psychological and ideological strength. His own heroic nature, however, is not allowed to overshadow his role in the struggle of the War of Liberation, and so his awareness of world revolution is increased.

In the play, the negative characters exist to highlight the heroic ones. The relationship between Mountain Vulture and Yang was redefined and Vulture appears as more of a foil for Yang's brilliance. Positive characters play roles that are at once equal and subordinate to Yang in value, creating a 'dialectical unity' whereby Yang is shown to be part of the masses and yet above them.

Modern revolutionary Peking Opera dispenses with traditional Confucian motivations like filial piety, righteousness, and loyalty in favor of a comprehensive sense of hostility. The proletariat is shown to have a vivid memory of the injustices inflicted by its class enemies, and a consuming passion to gain total revenge against them. This is brought out by presenting positive characters who have suffered severe physical and emotional defeats. Li Yung Chi's father was shot by Chiang Kai-shek's soldiers; he loses his wife in a bandit raid, and is himself captured. Hunter Chang and his daughter Bau have painful memories of a similar raid eight years earlier, where Chang's mother and wife lost their lives. Chang Bau is made to suffer the psychological burden of masquarading as a mute boy to avoid being captured.

The profound sense of shame at their inability to gain revenge leads to feelings of repressed hostility. The Communist party encourages these feelings – first, by emphasizing previous defeats and then by directing these feelings against class enemies. The party provides the only organized means whereby the proletariat can even the score and emerge securely victorious. Personal conversion is a prime action in revolutionary Peking Opera. The experience whereby a peasant, demoralized but sensitive to his social position, is awakened and rearmed with Mao Tse-tung's Thought is inevitably a turning point in the play.

The third scene presents Hunter Chang and Chang Bau living in a valley near Tiger Mountain. Having suffered in a bandit raid eight years before, they continue to live in fear, distrustful of any strangers. Yang Dz Rung is able to establish confidence with them and is the agent whereby Chang Bau is provoked to speak out and reveal their past. She sings several emotional arias, followed by Yang who encourages her to seek the Communist party as a 'savingstar.' When the Hunter and Chang Bau decide to help Yang defeat Mountain Vulture, the act becomes a complete presentation of the archetypal Communist experience. The party gains the sympathy of the proletariat, enlightens them, and joins with them to defeat the enemy. Based on the information supplied by Hunter Chang about the Agent's Map, Shau can begin to devise a strategy to capture Tiger Mountain. This pivotal act is designed to demonstrate Mao's dictum that the party depends on the masses in any struggle.

At some point before the final struggle, it is necessary to enlist more widespread support, demonstrated in Scene Seven. The arousal of the masses is represented by the conversion of Li Yung Chi. Li is extremely suspicious of the army and offers considerably more resistance than Hunter Chang. Lyu Hung Ye and Jung Jr Cheng both suffer temporary defeats when they are unable to overcome his antagonism. It remains for Shau Jyan Pwo to demonstrate the benevolence of the party. By extending medical attention to Mother Li and patient reasoning to Li, Shau overcomes Li's doubts. In a moving aria, Li expresses his new outlook. Once Li is won over, the other villagers join him onstage to display class unity. With the masses fully aroused, final plans for the attack can be made.

It is interesting to compare this play with the world of *The Wild Boar Forest* and note of how revolutionary Peking Opera has re-evaluated the image of the traditional heroic personality. The heroes of *Shwei Hu* live apart. Their singleminded emphasis on *yi* produces a lifestyle characterized by a sense of Romantic distortion, in basic conflict with the world around them. Mt. Lyang is bound together by a state of mind stressing sexual abstinence, the ability to indulge in a great amount of wine, loyalty to the brotherhood, strength, and personal courage. It is isolated, both physically and spiritually, from the outside world. Despite their brutality and bandit activities, the heroes have long appealed to Chinese audiences as men who follow their nature and live pure lives of free will.

In *Taking Tiger Mountain by Strategy*, the *Shwei Hu* legend is condemned by presenting a group of men analagous in many ways to the one hundred and eight heroes, but here they are the villains. Both groups see themselves as special communities linked by a sense of Brotherhood (*yi*). Members of such groups are supposed to recognize each other instinctively and form bonds of friendship. Yang Dz Rung appeals to this in Scene Six when he tries to join Mountain Vulture's band. Vulture, however, displays a commitment to *yi* that is, at best, unscrupulous. Greed for the Agent's Map and suspicion of all newcomers are the overiding thoughts in his mind. He is equally unable to distinguish between who is a member and who is not, for he trusts Yang and orders Lwan Ping killed.

In *Shwei Hu Jwan*, numerous feats of drinking are described. The hero shows his superiority to ordinary men by consuming tremendous quantities of wine without getting drunk. Lwan Ping, who ought to be considered a member of the Brotherhood, is discredited by having become drunk and allowing Yang to steal the Agent's Map from him. Mountain Vulture and the entire band are attacked and destroyed while indulging in the Hundred Chickens Feast.

Mountain Vulture's only motivation is rapacious lust for profit and fame. He lacks the hero's commitment to principle and the positive expression of the self. Moreover, he cannot be seen as a force of indignant righteousness in a corrupt and hostile world. The writers of the play were well aware that their characterization of Mountain Vulture borrowed key elements from the image of the Mt. Lyang heroes. But by presenting Yang Dz Rung as a new type of hero identified with the proletariat, Tiger Mountain and the Brotherhood become the enemies, not the allies, of the people. The band is discredited because they are tools of the feudal exploiting class, and because they fail to live up to their own implicit ideals.

The traditional heroic pose is criticized in modern, revolutionary Peking Opera for its crudity of manners and lack of political awareness. The new hero is the model Communist – modern, progressive, and efficient. Yet revolutionary opera has not freed itself entirely from traditional associations. Mountain Vulture's band must evoke the heroic community in order to reject the concept of *yi*.

In addition to preserving tradition as a useful foil, tradition can be used in positive ways, adding its remaining prestige to new concepts. In the sixth scene, Yang Dz Rung kills a tiger, and the action immediately calls to mind Chapter 23 of *Shwei Hu Jwan*. In one of the most famous episodes of Chinese fiction, the hero Wu Sung also kills a tiger in the mountains. Wu's virtues of bravery and strength still command enough respect in the Red Pear Garden to have the authors duplicate the incident in opera and link it to a proletarian hero. The purpose, it is explained, is to show that all reactionaries are 'paper tigers.'

Taking Tiger Mountain by Strategy is a translation of the October 1969 text as published in the party ideological journal, *Hung Chi*.[20] It was performed in commemoration of the twentieth anniversary of the founding of the People's Republic of China.

The three translations selected for this collection represent considerable latitude in approach and personal style. *The White Snake* attempts to capture the intricate rhythms of the Chinese in a subtle, poetic English. *Wild Boar Forest* concentrates on the sense of action in the plot, evoking the exuberant world of *Shwei Hu Jwan*. *Taking Tiger Mountain by Strategy* tries to maintain the sense of rhyme in the arias and to capture the fusion in the dialogue of traditional idioms and contemporary syntax. The very individual preferences of the translators testify to the wide range of possibilities offered by the Chinese originals.

1   Tang Ming Hwang reigned 713-755. In literature he is remembered for his patronage of the performing arts and for his love affair with the palace courtesan, Yang Kwei Fei. *See* Bwo Jyu Ui, *Song of Everlasting Lament;* Hung Sheng, *The Palace of Eternal Youth;* and the Peking Opera, *Kwei Fei Intoxicated.* The Yale system of romanizing Chinese names is used throughout this book, except for such familiar spellings as 'Mao Tse-tung.'

2   See the 'Records of Rites and Music' (*Li Ywe Jr*) in the *Tang History* (*Tang Shu*).

3   The Workshop was divided into the Right Section, which taught singing, and the Left Section, which gave instruction in dance. These institutions were responsible for developing new works, teaching them to the palace performers and preserving theatrical traditions. Though they played a diminished role in later times, the Workshops continued to exist until the fall of the Ching Dynasty in 1912. For a contemporary account see *Notes on the Music Workshop* (*Chyau Fang Ji*).

4   I follow the periodization of Jau Tsung in his *Jung Gwo Da Lu Di Syi Chyu Gai Ge* (*Theatre Reform on the Chinese Mainland*) *1942-1967* (Hong Kong: Jung Wen Da Sywe Chyu Ban She, 1969), except that I feel the outbreak of the Cultural Revolution should properly start a new period.

5   See an abridgement of Mao's 'Talks' in Bruno Shaw, ed., *Selected Works of Mao Tse-tung* (New York: Harper and Row, 1970), pp. 246-251.

6   *Ibid.,* p. 249.

7   During this period, however, a small number of highly successful plays were given wide exposure, at least in Peking and Shanghai. *The White Snake* by Tyan Han was one of these.

8   This statement was to be used against Tyan when he was attacked in 1966.

9   The first version of *Taking Tiger Mountain by Strategy* was among the many plays written then.

10 It was around this time that *Taking Tiger Mountain by Strategy* attracted Chiang Ch'ing's attention in Shanghai and she sponsored its re-editing.

11 See Clive Ansley's study, *The Heresy of Wu Han* (Toronto: University of Toronto Press, 1971), for a translation and study of the play *Hai Rwei's Dismissal.*

12 A *Tsz Hwa* is a short story form derived from the storyteller's art which combines poetry with vernacular narrative prose.

13 A variety of popular theatre in central China; normally sung by girl minstrels.

14 *Shwei Hu Jwan* was translated as *The Water Margin* by J. H. Jackson and as *All Men Are Brothers* by Pearl S. Buck.

15 For a study of *Shwei Hu Jwan, see* Richard Irwin's *The Evolution of a Chinese Novel* (Cambridge, Mass.: Harvard University Press, 1966).

16 C. T. Hsia gives a critical analysis of the novel in *The Classic Chinese Novel* (New York: Columbia University Press, 1968), chap. 3.

17 *Ibid.*, p. 89.

18 *Taking Tiger Mountain by Strategy* Section, 'Strive to Create the Brilliant Images of Proletarian Heroes,' *Chinese Literature*, 1 (1970) 58, 59.

19 *See* Shaw, *Selected Works of Mao Tse-tung*, p. 328, for an abridged text of the instructions.

20 See *Hung Chi*, 11 (1969), 32-61 for a complete text in Chinese. An English translation appeared in *Chinese Literature*, 1 (1970) 3-57.

THE STAGING OF PEKING OPERA

by John D. Mitchell and Donald Chang

The three plays of *The Red Pear Garden* illustrate different stages in the development of Peking Opera: the traditional play; the play that uses elements of Western stage practice (a tendency that began in China as early as 1911); and the post-Cultural Revolution opera that breaks with the traditional staging. Even the last example, however, shows evidence of the patterns, techniques, and style of the early teahouse open stage.

The actor is central in Chinese theatre. The platform stage, with the audience on three sides of the old teahouse, was smaller than Shakespeare's thrust stage, but not dissimilar. Almost nothing except the actor appeared on the stage. At the rear of the platform was a richly embroidered hanging; a vertical slit to the left and a vertical slit to the right provided for entrances and exits. The pattern was rigid: actors always entered from audience left and exited from audience right.

A table and two chairs made up the basic stage furniture. Each was draped with an embroidered cloth. The simple combination of a table and chairs could be used during the play as a table and chairs or as a city wall, or a mountain or throne. Great ingenuity was practiced in using these simple stage properties for the needs and the action of the drama. No curtain existed in the traditional Chinese playhouse; the property man, dressed in a long, dark gown, would rearrange the furniture in view of the audience. When a change was required – for example, from an indoor scene during which two characters had been seated at a table – as soon as the actors exited the property man walked onstage and rearranged the properties to serve as a mountain or whatever the next scene required. Either the dialogue of the entering actors or the rearranged properties, with perhaps an appropriate banner, told the audience immediately of the change of scene. The stage lighting for traditional plays was unchanging; it was simply the brightest amount of light available for lighting the actors on stage.

When hand props, such as whips or swords, were needed, the property man arrived on stage and handed them to the actors, even in the midst of a battle. Few hand properties were used, other than knives, daggers, spears, swords, banners, whips, or batons. The horse whip was an important hand property. A baton with tufts of fringe, it indicated that the actor carrying it was riding a horse. Mime was used instead of most hand props, and this illustrates another dimension of the Peking Opera: the traditional Chinese actor was a master of mime.

In the traditional Chinese theatre, dating from the platform stage of the old teahouse, the orchestra of six to eight musicians was located downstage, audience right. It consisted of traditional Chinese strings and percussions. Its placement onstage was not arbitrary. The closest of relationships existed between the musicians and the performers; the pacing of the performance, however, was invariably determined by the actor.

Scholars have pointed out that the music of Peking Opera is largely the creation of the actors. This is not surprising, since it has been noted repeatedly that in this traditional theatre the actor is central. What is called Peking Opera in the West is known as *jing syi*, or capitol drama, to the Chinese. Unlike Western opera it is not primarily a vehicle for orchestral or vocal music; it is drama throughout which there are arias and, from time to time, musical accompaniment to the action. The arias are delivered in what approximates a *bel canto* style; they are still another means by which the actor may show his virtuosity. All the last words of the lines of each aria must rhyme. Melodies are created in compliance with the tones of the Chinese words. There are whole categories of beats.

All operas contain *approximately* the same tunes. Characters of any category may sing any tune; i.e. there are no restrictions on which characters sing which tunes. All the notes in the musical scale are used, as in the West, although *fa* and *ti* are rarely used, except when expressing sadness. There are at least five musicians: two playing two-string violins (*hu*) and three playing percussion (*lwo gu:* gongs and drums); they operate in close association with the performers. In contrast to Western music, tempos and beats may vary at the performer's will; certain notes may be prolonged as deemed necessary. Thus, performers and musicians must have intensive rehearsals, and the latter take cues from the former when on stage.

There are about twenty tunes found in all Chinese operas, called *ban*. Each has specific characteristics and is used in a particular situation. The Chinese character for *ban* means board or beat; it originated in early times, it is believed, when accompaniment was primitive and a board was used to beat out the rhythm and accompany the tune. Despite its literal translation, *ban* is best understood as both beat and tune. The most frequently used beats are:

1 DAU[1] BAN (lead-beat): always one line only, an introductory singing line leading to the next singing beat; no set rhythm.

2 YWAN BAN (basic beat): slow $\frac{4}{4}$ beat used mainly for narrative soliloquies; slower tunes (e.g. *ywan ban* and *man ban*), three *eyes* and one *board* (three beats plus one accented beat).

3 MAN BAN (slow beat): identical to *ywan ban* except sung somewhat more slowly; an actor may substitute one for the other to suit him or her personally.

4 KWAI BAN (fast beat): a regular but very fast beat, used mainly for showing anxiety or anger; faster tunes, only *boards*, no *eyes* (consistent accented beats).

5 LYOU SHWEI (flowing water): almost as fast as *kwai ban*, also one consistent tempo.

6 SAN BAN (loose beat): irregular; every note may be shortened or prolonged as the performer improvises; uniquely, faster music accompanies slower singing; the first singing note of each line must fall on a musical note.

7 YAU BAN (shake beat): very much like *san ban*, no set tempo, improvised by singers; one deviation affects the other: music and singing are uniformly slow.

The four basic keys are indicated for all the beats. They vary in both origin and pitch, and are placed before the *ban* when the complete terminology is used. They are:

1 SYI PI (western skin): the two-string violin is usually tuned for *la* and *mi* (with the latter in a range one octave higher than the former).

2 ER HWANG (two-string): violin is tuned for *sol* and *re* (the latter in a range one octave higher).

3   FAN ER HWANG (reversed two-string): mainly used for passages of sadness.

4   FAN SYI PI (reversed western skin): rarely used.

Thus, for a complete musical designation of any aria in any opera, one must say, for example, *syi pi ywan ban, syi pi lyou shwei, er hwang yau ban,* or *er hwang man ban.* Generally a connoisseur may spot a *ban* readily, yet he has to listen to the lyrics to tell which opera the aria is from. However, some arias from certain operas have distinguishable characteristics owing to note changes and the like, so they become quite different from other arias with the same *ban.* But these are considered exceptions to the rule.

The literal translation of the Chinese characters for some of these *ban* designations provides the layman – even the Chinese layman – with little clue to their meaning. Murky as the terms are – one thinks of the French terminology used worldwide in classical ballet – they do have precise meaning for the theatre musicians and actors. Each has its own fixed tune, structure, mode, rhythm, and tempo. In rehearsing and performing with the musicians, the actors dictate the tempo and sometimes the key. Modern revolutionary Peking Opera has assimilated various styles of singing from traditional Peking Opera, making many creative changes to suit the portrayal of the proletarian heroes.

Western authorities are of the opinion that Western musical notation can arrive at only an approximation of the music of Peking Opera. Raymond Hargrave, who was music director for IASTA's production of *The White Snake,* does believe that the Western ear is able to hear quarter tones. And the professional Chinese actress Hu Hung Yen feels that Chinese theatre music and Peking Opera can be rendered fully in Western notation. They both agree that individual style presents a challenge to the performer. When the singing actor of the West essays the performance of Peking Opera in English, he will find the Western notation helpful, but he must be content to hope for, at best, an evocation of the original. When the Institute for Advanced Studies in the Theatre Arts produced Japanese Noh and Kabuki in English, the actors were advised by the professional Broadway musical director James Leon to aim for a *styling* of the Asian music, grounded in Western notation.

Peking Opera is popular theatre. Ninety percent of the audience is usually familiar with the play. They attend not to be startled or entertained by the novelty of a new story but to savor, as connoisseurs, the skill of the performer: his singing, his gestures and movements, his versatility. Indeed, the stories tend to be old and familiar. The theatre is also a gathering place for meeting friends and conversing. Food is available and during the performance wines and teas are served. It is a social occasion. When a Western person first enters a Chinese theatre, he is likely to be amazed by the amount of conversation going on during the performance, as well as the presence of all members of the family, including small children and babies. Nevertheless, when an actor has arrived at a familiar and loved scene, or if the actor is in top form, all activity and commotion in the audience will cease. One can hear a pin drop.

The actor is central, and the color and richness of fabric of the costumes enhance him, his gestures, and his movements. The costumes serve a fundamentally theatrical purpose, and they are not necessarily accurate historically. There is the one exception: characters in any opera taking place at the time of the Ching Dynasty, when the Manchus ruled China, would wear the recognizable and distinct costume of the Manchu people. Stories taking place before the time of the Ching Dynasty use the same costume regardless of dynasty or period. The costumes have evolved in relation to the character and the demands of the acting, singing, and acrobatics of the role.

Roles are far less diverse than in Western theatre, and are easily identified on the Peking Opera stage. Just as the Chinese audience for Peking Opera is not concerned with the plot but rather with the expertise of the acting, so too it is not interested in the subtlety of naturalistic individual characterization. The characters are stereotypes. This does not disturb the Chinese audience, but actually contributes to the immediate recognition of the role that the actor is playing in the story.

There are four main categories of roles. The first comprises genteel male characters, known in Chinese theatre as *sheng:* they may be young (*syau sheng*) or old (*lau sheng*); scholars (*wen sheng*) or warriors (*wu sheng*). A second category would be female characters, known as *dan:* they may be fragile (*ching yi*); coquettish maidens (*hwa dan*); or female warriors (*wu dan*).

The category of more mature, exuberant male characters is known as *jing*. They are also popularly known as painted face characters or *hwa lyan,* because the actor makes up his face into brightly colored patterns which change his face to resemble a mask, and from the choice of colors the audience is able to determine immediately if he is a villain or a hero. They may be old or young, and quite a number of them are warriors. The fourth and last category comprises the clown characters, known to the Chinese audiences as *chou:* a distinct characteristic of this category is the cloverleaf, white patch of makeup around the actor's eyes and nose. The makeup produces a comic effect and the character may, in that respect, play a part resembling the clown roles of plays in the West; but he may also be a central character in a play, and even a villain.

In *The White Snake,* Lady White and her companion are in the *dan* stereotype or category; Syu Syan, the young lover of White, is the *syau sheng* type of the *sheng* category of characters. The priest Fa Hai is of the *jing* category, although not a 'painted face' character.

The Wild Boar Forest also observes the traditional categories of characters. The young, spoiled son of the Minister of War, Gau Shr De – the villain of the piece – surprisingly for the Western audience comes out of the clown category or the *chou* stereotype. It does not make him less of a villain, but it does enable him to elicit laughs from time to time from the audience. Lin Chung is a warrior or *wu sheng* stereotype from the *sheng* category; his blood-brother, the monk Lu Jr Shen, is a true 'painted face' or *hwa lyan* type from the *jing* category. The four ruffians, who later become the followers of Lu Jr Shen, like Gau Shr De, are clown or *chou* stereotypes.

Certain plays of the Peking Opera repertory may be referred to as genteel plays (*sheng* plays) because the *sheng* character dominates the action of this play; another play is likely to be referred to as a coquette play because the coquette or *hwa dan* plays the leading role; by the same token other plays are referred to as painted face plays (*hwa lyan* plays) or clown plays (*chou* plays). Just as the differing categories of characters have distinct personalities, so does the style of singing vary from category to category. The young genteel character sings falsetto, which, on first encounter, falls most strangely upon Western ears. At the other extreme are the painted face characters who have developed extraordinarily large, booming, orotund vocal qualities. Female characters sing in high-pitched voices. The clowns are more likely to be cracking jokes than singing. Clowns also are likely to use the colloquial Peking dialect and to make direct reference from time to time to the audience. The vocabulary of stylish gesture is lengthy, highly developed, and elaborate; by comparison it suggests the vocabulary of Western classical ballet.

When the story turns to a scene of fighting, not only the central characters but also extra actors may appear on stage and perform feats of sword play and acrobatics. The versatility of the Chinese performer is essential. He begins his training at an early age, and it has been customary for him to live at the theatrical school. Long hours are devoted to learning and to performing. It is traditional for the actors to commit to memory the repertory of plays that are likely to be their life's work – not only the lines of dialogue and the arias, but the gestures and movements, acrobatics and sword play. They learn not only their own roles, but the complete texts of the plays. A mature actor in Peking Opera may have a hundred plays memorized, but from his youth has been committed to playing, usually, only one category of roles. Formerly, a number of male actors had been trained to perform a female role as well.

Plays written before 1911 are known as traditional plays. They follow most austerely the conventions of the old teahouse stage. After 1911 new plays were written, although the stories were derived from myths and classic novels. The style of singing, the costuming, and the categories of characters remained the same, but backdrops began to be used as scenery. *The White Snake* uses a minimum of backdrops.

After 1949 more plays were written (although still based on historical events), more elaborate backdrops appeared, lighting effects were used, and stage properties and elements of scenery were introduced. *Wild Boar Forest* illustrates this transitional type of Peking Opera, using greater elements of scenery, undoubtedly stimulated by the theatre practice of the West. During this transitional period, the orchestra moved from its place onstage to the wings of the theatre, out of view of the audience.

The plays came to be performed in theatres that resembled the proscenium-type theatre of the West, and greater use was made of both act curtains and upstage curtains, permitting changes of scenery out the audience's view. In *Wild Boar Forest* the familiar property man has disappeared.

Since the Cultural Revolution, the People's Republic of China has accelerated the introduction of naturalistic staging for the revolutionary operas. In addition to the creation of ideal class heroes, technical changes in Peking Opera have been made. Under the principles of 'Prominence to the Prominent, Conciseness of Expression for the Benefit of the Masses, and Distinctiveness in Shades,' the language has been made more colloquial for the heroes, while evil characters preserve the accents and voice modulations that sound antiquated and sinister.[2] Revolutionary Peking Opera mixes the two basic modes of *syi pi* and *er hwang* in the same set of arias. The percussion, traditionally an arrangement of stereotyped patterns, is modified, especially in Scene Five. Traditional role categories have been abolished entirely. Revolutionary Peking Opera deals with the world of proletarian resistance and uses the more obvious division of good and evil classes. Certain arias were traditionally restricted to particular roles, and with the disappearance of these roles, various types of music are used more widely. Indeed, the music itself has been altered by the inclusion of Western instruments in the orchestra. In addition to the traditional *er hu* and *hu chin* violins and the moon guitar, Western violins, pianos, and percussion, arranged in orchestra fashion, are used, all the result of 'the assimilation of foreign progressive culture.'[3]

What had started as theatre criticism expanded into a vast political struggle, which had its consequences for the Red Pear Garden. Full attention was turned on modern, revolutionary Peking Opera and its typical elements were formalized. No longer were characters to be cast in the traditional roles of *sheng, dan, jing* and *chou*. Old rules about the use of certain arias and singing styles according to roles were abandoned. New costumes appropriate to peasants, workers, and soldiers dominated the stage. Old mannerisms and dancing were either modified or dropped entirely in favor of a more active choreography. Realistic scenery and Western stage effects were used exclusively. In 1965, an article that grew out of a Central China conference

urged that modern, revolutionary Peking Opera occupy the entire repertory, and it was reported that both Mao Tse-tung and
Chiang Ch'ing favored a permanent ban on traditional opera.
Taking Tiger Mountain by Strategy is an example of modern,
revolutionary Peking Opera.

1 The layman, both Western and Chinese, has often been misled in translating the Chinese character *dau*, because in early times an arbitrary character was set down to represent the sound *dau*. Today that character would be translated as *reverse*, but to theatre musicians, even though it is an inaccurate character, it means *lead*.

2 Art Troupe of Peking Garrison Forces: Brilliant Example of the Revolution in Peking Opera Music *Chinese Literature*, 2 (1970), 92.

3 Two helpful sources on Chinese music are: Walter Kaufman, *Musical Notations of the Orient* (Bloomington, Ind., Indiana University Press, 1967); and A. C. Scott, *The Classical Theatre of China* (London: Allen & Unwin, 1957).

TYAN HAN

The White Snake

TRANSLATED BY DONALD CHANG
ENGLISH VERSE ADAPTATION BY
WILLIAM PACKARD

CHARACTERS

LADY WHITE (Bai Su Jen) a white snake spirit who takes the form of a young woman

LITTLE BLUE a blue snake spirit, companion to Lady White

SYU SYAN a young scholar from Jen Jyang

FA HAI High Priest from the Golden Mountain Temple

MRS CHEN Syu Syan's elder sister

BOATMAN

FA MING, FOLLOWERS AND GUARDS from the Golden Mountain Temple

NOVICE MONK from the Golden Mountain Temple

WEI TWO a disciple of Fai Hai

HOLY OLD MAN FROM THE SOUTH a god in heaven

DEER BOY, CRANE BOY guardians of the holy mushrooms

WATER ANIMALS

WIND GOD

TOWER GOD guardian of Thunder Peak Pagoda

PLACE NAMES

WEST LAKE — where Su Jen White meets Syu Syan; near Hang Chou

MOUNT O-MEI — place of spirits; home of White and Blue

RIVER SOUTH — the Yangtze; where White and Blue now live

BAU SHU TOWER
SU BREAKWATER — all at West Lake
BROKEN BRIDGE

LWO YANG — where heroine from love story met Pan An

CHING PWO GATE — where Syu Syan lives; in city of Jen Jyang

SHRINE OF KING OF CHYAN — outside Ching Pwo Gate

TSAU SHRINE — near Chyan Tang Gate

MOUNT LING YIN — burial place of Syu Syan's mother

GOLDEN MOUNTAIN TEMPLE — Fa Hai's temple

JEN JYANG — city where both Syu Syan and Su Jen White live

HANG JOU — city from which Syu Syan first came

BAU HE HALL — name of herb shop owned by White and Syu Syan

MOUNT DUNG TING — where fruit came from that Syu bought

HOLY MOUNTAIN — Pang Lai, legendary mountain where Su Jen White travels to steal the Holy Mushrooms

JAU LIN PALACE — at Holy Mountain

WEN SHU HALL — meditation hall inside Golden Mountain Temple

LIN AN — home of Syu Syan's sister

THUNDER PEAK PAGODA — Where Su Jen White is taken to remain for several hundred years

CHYAN TANG RIVER — river near Lei Feng Tower; connected to West Lake

CHINESE RHYME ENDINGS	ENGLISH EQUIVALENTS
an	ē (ā) (and)
ang	and
au	ē
wo	ā
ai	ear
ei	ows (ake, owers)
eng	ake (owers)
en	ife
in	ice (ove, ome, ace)
ing	eyes (ill, use)
wu	ays
yu	ī (grave)
ou	oo
ung	ouls
yi	old (storm)
dz	child
e	earth
a	e
tsz	eer

IMPERFECT RHYMES MAY OCCUR BETWEEN THE FOLLOWING PAIRS

an – ang

en – eng

an – en

ang – eng

wo – e

en – in

eng – ing

ai – ei

yi – ei

yi – yu

an – in

SCENE 1 *Strolling by West Lake*

WHITE *offstage*
We take the southern way from O-mei.   9, an

Enter SU JEN WHITE *and* LITTLE BLUE

We can see great lakes and tall mountains today,   11, an
and we can see Bau Shu pagoda in these calm waves,   13, an
also a stately archway by those three lakes.   11, an
Su Jou willows embrace the boats that sway,   10, an
a chill wind makes peach and plum blossoms shake.   10, an

BLUE Sister, I'm so glad we came here. There's so much to see – boys and girls go strolling in pairs beside West Lake.

WHITE When you and I were together, were practicing spiritual matters, our place was high and cold – each day we were hidden in white clouds, and each day we walked along the trail; all we saw was horse chestnut flowers. Now, coming to the south of the river, we see how warm and soft the hills are – how happy they make me feel! Sister Blue, come see! That bridge ahead of us – it must be the famous Broken Bridge.

BLUE But Sister, if it is called Broken Bridge, then why isn't it broken?

WHITE Sister Blue,

Broken Bridge is what people always say.   10, an
In two's and three's they cross the bridge each day.   10, an
Somehow their troubles seem to go away.   10, an
This sight is worth the trip from far O-mei.   10, an

The sky darkens suddenly

Oh, no! Suddenly the wind grows wild, the sky turns gray!

BLUE Sister, look! Over there is a man with an umbrella under his arm, a handsome man!

WHITE Where? Oh!

Just like a hero out of yesterday!   10, an

BLUE *seeing that* WHITE *is staring at* SYU SYAN
It's raining – let's go, Sister.

WHITE Yes, let's go –

My heart has waves that never went astray,   10, an
yet why do they all run so wild today?   10, an

BLUE *tries to keep* WHITE *out of the rain.* SYU SYAN *enters, carrying an open umbrella*

SYU I prayed at my mother's grave.   7, yu
A great storm begins to rave.   7, yi
Willow leaves say wave to wave,   7, yi
peach flowers break, small and brave.   7, ei
No time to see fair sights today.   8, yi

BLUE Sister, it's raining harder. Let's get under this willow tree.

WHITE All right.

SYU *sees the two women under the willow tree*

SYU Oh!

They should not stay in the rain.   7, yi

Turns to the women

Ladies, where are you going?

BLUE My mistress and I were out walking by the lake when this storm came up. We want to return to Chyan Tang Gate. May I ask where are you going?

SYU I am going to Ching Pwo Gate. How can you hide there under a willow tree during such a rain storm? Please use my umbrella.

WHITE But what about you?

SYU It does not matter about me.

WHITE But that's not right.

BOATMAN *offstage*
Long oars make a great white wake.   7, ei
I take guests to watch plums shake.   7, ei

SYU The rain is getting worse – ladies, let me call the boat.

WHITE Very well, thank you.

She takes the umbrella

SYU You're welcome.

BOATMAN *appearing with boat*
I have bought some wine to make   7, ei
me drunk out there on the lake.   7, ei

SYU Hey, boatman!

BOATMAN Do you want a boat?

SYU That's right.

BOATMAN Where do you want to go?

SYU First take these ladies to Chyan Tang Gate, and then you can take me to Ching Pwo Gate – I will pay you well.

BOATMAN All right, get aboard.

SYU Put the handles on.

BOATMAN Be careful, the floor of the boat is slippery.

WHITE Little Blue, help me!

SYU *also aboard*
All right, let's go!

He stays at the other end of the boat, and uses his sleeve to keep the rain away

BOATMAN The wind is strong; you should stay very close together.

BLUE That's right, it's raining harder. Let's all use the umbrella.

SYU *declining*
That's all right.

WHITE That's really not right!

Blue goes over to cover SYU SYAN *with the umbrella, leaving* WHITE *half exposed in the rain.* BLUE *moves back a little, thus causing* WHITE *and* SYU SYAN *to come closer together, reluctantly.*

BOATMAN These are good days on West Lake,   7, an
as we go through wind and rain –   7, an
ten lifetimes to meet a mate,   7, an
then a hundred to embrace.   7, an

WHITE *and* SYU SYAN *look at each other; the sky suddenly becomes clear, and* SYU SYAN *draws away slightly*

SYU Good, it's stopped raining.

Now the sky is clear above the lake –   9, an
all my clothes are soaked with rain.   7, an

BLUE My Lady, look, the storm is over, the sky is clear. West Lake looks wonderful!

WHITE Yes!

The lake and sky are both washed clear;   8, yi
a spring breeze blows through me here.   7, yi

SYU *with great feeling*
Now West Lake begins to appear,   8, dz
like this lady, fair and dear   7, yi

WHITE Blue,

ask the man if he lives near here,   8, yi
we should call and wish him cheer.   7, yi

BLUE Yes. Sir, where do you live? My Lady wants to thank you.

SYU Oh no, that is too kind.

I live beyond the Ching Pwo Gate,   8, ai
west of Chyan shrine, which is near,   7, yi
but it is a poor place I fear,   8, yi
too lowly for your lovely sake.   8, ei

WHITE *seeing that* SYU SYAN *is silent*
He's being modest.

He is so humble and sincere,   8, yi
he is so silent and so dear –   8, yi
ask him again; make it clear   7, yi
he must come to Tsau Shrine near here.   8, tsz

BLUE Yes – Sir, we live near Tsau Shrine outside Chyan Tang Gate.
The red building is our Lady's place. You must come to visit us
sometime.

SYU The Lady lives near Tsau Shrine. I shall pay a visit someday.

BOATMAN Here we are, at Chyan Tang Gate.

WHITE *holds the umbrella and looks at* SYU SYAN *longingly; he
returns the look.* BLUE *points at the sky, which immediately
darkens*

BLUE Oh, it's raining again!

Rain comes down

WHITE Yes, it is raining again. What shall we do?

BLUE It is a nuisance! this umbrella –

SYU The Lady may keep the umbrella, I will come get it some other day.

WHITE Thank you, sir –

with kindness, I thank you.	6, ang
Chyan Tang Gate: our trip is through.	7, ang

– Sir, please look:

My house, see, there's a good view,	7, ang
it wants a visit from you.	7, ang
Please, help me get ashore now, Blue!	8, ang

BLUE *turning back and looking at* SYU SYAN
You must come tomorrow!

SYU I will go to visit you tomorrow. Lady, please walk slowly and be careful.

WHITE Goodbye, good sir.

It will break my heart if you do not come soon.	11, ang

Slight glance, exits with BLUE

SYU *watching them walk away*
What a lovely Lady!

Like a goddess going home.	7, ang

He remembers

Oh!

I did not ask for her name.	7, ang

To BLUE

Little Lady, turn around.

BLUE   What is the matter? Do you want the umbrella?

SYU   No, no. I want to know the name of your Lady.

BLUE   My Lady's name is White.

SYU   I see. And do you know my name?

BLUE   You, sir? It's Syu, isn't it?

SYU   That's right. But how did you know?

BLUE   Syu is written right on your umbrella. Sir, please do come soon, so my Lady will not have long to wait.

SYU   Yes, I will. Now please be careful.

BLUE   Goodbye.

  BLUE *turns and exits*

SYU   *looking after* BLUE
  Ha ha ha . . .

  What a rare and clever little lady.   10, ang
  Like the lady's red maiden.   7, ang

  In ecstasy he forgets

  Oh, what is the lady's name? It's . . .

BOATMAN   *dryly*
  It's White.

SYU   That's right, it's White.

BOATMAN Don't tell me that after all of this, you don't even know her. I thought you were from the same family.

SYU Well, that's why they say, 'strangers until we meet each other.'

BOATMAN In a storm, all are brothers.   7, a

He begins to move the boat, startling SYU

Passenger, please be careful.

SYU *looks at the shore as the boat exits*

SCENE 2 *Getting Married*

At a red building by the lake

BLUE *offstage*
I sweep away sweet flowers   7, eng
To receive the handsome man now.   8, en

This way please, Mr Syu. *Leads* SYU SYAN *onstage*

To SYU

Mr Syu, please sit down.

She exits

SYU This is a heavenly place,   7, ing
by the water's open space.   8, in

BLUE *leads in* WHITE

WHITE What is it?

BLUE *whispers*
He is here.

WHITE *with joy*
Ah, where is he? He is . . .

SYU How are you?

WHITE How are you? Please do sit down.

They sit. BLUE *serves tea*

WHITE There was so much rain yesterday on the lake. If you had not been there to lend us your umbrella and call the boat for us, it would have been so bad for Blue and me.

SYU It is a gentleman's duty to do what he can do, so please do not mention it at all.

WHITE Blue, serve wine. I'll drink a cup or two to show my thanks to the gentleman.

BLUE Yes. *She exits*

SYU I am causing you too much trouble.

WHITE Not at all.

BLUE *appears with cups on a plate, and she pours the wine*

WHITE I salute you, sir.

SYU And I salute you, my Lady.

WHITE May I ask if you have a family?

SYU I lost both my parents when I was a child, and so I have been living in my older sister's home. Although my brother-in-law treats me well enough, he is not wealthy. But through his help, I have begun to work in an herb shop, selling medicines.

WHITE   Since you work in an herb shop selling medicines, how could you have time to go strolling by the lake yesterday?

SYU   Oh no, I was not strolling by the lake at all. My dear mother is buried behind Ling Yin Mountain. Yesterday was the anniversary of the day she died, and so I asked for half a day to go and pay my respects at her grave. The rains came when I passed by the Su Breakwater on my way home. That was when I was lucky enough to meet you.

WHITE   Your devotion to your dear mother is truly beautiful.

She lifts her wine cup

Please.

SYU   Please.

WHITE *takes a sip, stands up softly, pulls* BLUE

WHITE   Blue!

BLUE   Yes, my Lady.

WHITE   Let me speak to you. *She whispers to* BLUE

BLUE   Oh no, I would be too embarrassed to ask.

WHITE *tugs at* BLUE's *dress eagerly*

Couldn't you two simply talk face to face?

WHITE   Dear Sister, do me this favor, please . . . WHITE *shakes her sleeves, exits*

BLUE   Scholar Syu, my Lady wants me to ask if you have ever been married?

SYU   I have always been alone. I have never even thought of marriage.

BLUE   Mr Syu, since you have no one, and since my Lady is not mar-
       ried, and since both of us have no one to rely on, my Lady thinks
       that you might join with her and live together as husband and
       wife. Now how would you feel about that?

SYU   If she would be my wife, I would be greatly honored. But I just
       told you, I work in an herb shop selling medicines, and I have to
       live on a very small income. How could I support the two of
       you?

BLUE   My Lady and I have never worried about our food and lodging.
       When my late Master passed away, he left my Lady a small
       fortune. Since you work in an herb shop selling medicines, and
       since my Lady also knows all about herbs and medicines, you
       could form a pair and work together, so why should you worry?

SYU   I should go home and tell my sister.

BLUE   What is the hurry? Wouldn't it be more exciting to introduce
       your new wife to her sister and brother-in-law after the wedding
       ceremony?

SYU   There's only one thing – this has all happened so suddenly, I
       don't have any wedding gift with me.

BLUE   Who needs a wedding gift! Besides, that umbrella of yours is the
       best wedding gift there could be. Today is a lucky day for mar-
       riages, so why don't you two do it, as soon as I light the wedding
       candles. *She lights the candles*

SYU   But – But –

BLUE   Everything is ready, so let me recite a few lines of praise:

Lovers come from distant lands;	7, an
like white lilies their love stands.	7, an
Tonight lovers will join hands,	7, ai
gods will bless their wedding bands.	7, an

       Now for some music, and I will bring out the bride.

Music begins in an adjacent room. BLUE *makes* SYU *stand facing the East, then she hurries out to bring* WHITE *in.* WHITE *is in a red gown and floral crown. She steps in gingerly.* BLUE *takes her to* SYU SYAN *and they all bow to each other*

BLUE *bowing, reciting*
 To all good gods   4, yi
 you both must bow.   4, ang
 Husband and wife   4, ai
 together now.   4, ang

The ceremony is thus performed, and BLUE *sends* WHITE *and* SYU SYAN *to the bedroom*

SCENE 3 *The Investigation*

At the Golden Mountain Temple. FA HAI *sits on the mattress, chanting. His followers stand.*

FOLLOWERS We have seen men rise and fall.   7, ang
     All things seek peace after all.   7, ang

FA HAI I laugh at life, for I see   7, an
   Men are lost and so unfree.   7, an
   I teach the true way to be –   7, an
   Turning towards serenity.   7, an

I am the old priest Fa Hai, who lives at Golden Mountain. Recently, there came to Jen Jyang one Su Jen White. I myself investigated her, and I have found out that she is really the incarnation of a snake spirit who has existed for a thousand years. She seduced Syu Syan of Hang Jou, married him, and began to work in an herb shop selling medicines there. This Buddhist's land all around the south of the river has no place for an evil demon spirit who has come to spoil and poison everything. In all conscience, I must rescue Syu Syan and destroy this White woman. I sent Fa Ming to get more information for me; I wonder why he has not come back with his report.

FA MING *enters*

FA MING My respects to you, my Master.

FA HAI What did you learn about White and Syu?

FA MING I saw Syu Syan. I asked him for some alms, and he gave me some herbs.

FA HAI You should have asked him to come and see me.

FA MING I said to Syu Syan: 'On the fifteenth day of this month, the Goddess of Mercy of our temple will give us her holy rays, and my Master has asked me to come and ask you to give us the honor of your presence in our temple for incense burning.' Syu Syan was about to say something, when Little Blue, the maid of Su Jen White, interrupted him, saying: 'These are my Lady's words: "We do not want to have anything to do with either Buddhists or Taoists. Even if Fa Hai himself were to come here, we would never go." '

FA HAI This is irritating!

On this holy land I see   7, an
demons speak absurdity.   7, an

He changes his clothes and gets his walking stick

So now it is up to me   7, an
to go and get Syu Syan free.   7, an

FOLLOWERS Goodbye, Master.

FA HAI Goodbye. *He exits*

SCENE 4   *Persuading Syu Syan*

Inside Bau He Hall

SYU   I bought some fruit on my way,   7, wo
       to give my Lady today.   7, wo

Blue enters

BLUE   Master, you have come home.

SYU   Yes. Where is your Lady?

BLUE   My Lady is still seeing patients.

WHITE   *offstage*
       Now I want you to go home and be well.

LADY
PATIENT   *offstage*
       All my thanks, Lady.

WHITE   Be careful, watch your step!

She enters

       Oh, my husband, you have come home.

SYU   That's right. Dear Lady, you must be tired, please try to rest.

He hides the fruit basket

WHITE   When I see a patient, I simply cannot rest.

SYU   But don't forget, you are going to have a baby.

WHITE   *shyly*
       I know that. *She sees the fruit basket* What is that?

SYU   As I came by the river, I saw some fresh fruit from Dung Ting
       Mountain, so I brought some home for you.

WHITE Sometimes you are too thoughtful. *She takes some fruit* Thank
you.

     SYU *puts the fruit basket on the table, takes his wife by the arm*

SYU Please don't say that I am too thoughtful. You know that I was
an orphan and that I have been alone all my life. It has only been
since I met you that I have known any happiness. Now that we
have settled in Jen Jyang, with your help, the herb shop has
begun to flourish, and I cannot begin to tell you how grateful I
am to you!

My dear wife, you are so sincere.   8, ai

Blue!

BLUE Yes, Master.

SYU Go and ask Mr Dou to see to the patients, so our Lady can get
some rest.

BLUE Yes. *She exits*

SYU Come, my Lady . . .
It is time for us to go to bed, my dear.   11, ai

He smiles, exits

WHITE My dear husband, I am coming right away . . .

Syu has been good to me since we came here.   10, ai
We share our joys, we calm each other's fears.   10, ei
Just now I feel the joy of earth appear,   10, ei
River South has given me these good years.   10, ei

     SYU SYAN *re-enters*

SYU Why haven't you come to bed?

WHITE I am coming.

She holds SYU SYAN *lovingly, about to exit to bedroom.* BLUE *enters from left*

BLUE   Master, Mr Dou will do what you say.

BLUE *exits with them. Moments later,* FA HAI *enters with a stick in his hand*

FA HAI   I've come miles, with stick in hand,   7, ang
seeking demons through the land.   7, ang

Is there anyone in the store?

SYU SYAN *enters, looking for fruit basket, and he greets* FA HAI

SYU   Oh Master, how are you?

FA HAI   How are you? Are you Mr Syu?

SYU   Yes. may I ask your name?

FA HAI   I am the High Priest Fa Hai.

SYU   Ah, you are the Master Priest Fa Hai. You must have come for alms, but I have already given some herbs.

FA HAI   That was good of you. However, I am not here today for alms.

SYU   Then you must have come as a patient, but my wife is very tired and she is trying to rest.

FA HAI   Please do not disturb her. My purpose in coming here is to take care of your own illness.

SYU   But I am not ill.

FA HAI *looking at* SYU
I can see your face is full of evil, and that is because you have been captured by demons. How can you say you are not ill?

SYU   Where is this demon you are speaking of?

FA HAI Right by your own side.

SYU *is startled and looks around.*

SYU I don't see any.

FA HAI Mr. Syu, forgive me if I am plain. *He whispers* I myself have investigated, and I have found out that your wife is really the incarnation of a snake spirit who has existed for a thousand years.

SYU Oh no – my wife is a very kind and gentle person. How could she be the incarnation of a snake spirit who has existed for a thousand years? You are extremely rude to say a thing like that.

FA HAI Mr Syu, it is only because I know that you are noble in your soul, that I myself came here from the Golden Mountain to talk to you. If you do not wake up in time, I am afraid that you will be destroyed.

SYU But if she is trying to destroy me, why is she so very kind and gentle to me?

FA HAI That is so she can get hold of you, and then when the right moment comes, she will devour you.

SYU Do you mean to say the way she works so hard – how she forgets to eat her meals, just so she can take care of all her patients – do you mean to say that this is so she can charm me out of my senses?

FA HAI Well . . .

Mr Syu, you must not refuse to wake:	10, eng
I say that your Lady is a demon snake,	11, eng
And I'm telling you this for your own sake.	10, eng
She will destroy your life, make no mistake.	10, en

SYU Master Priest,

Lady White is my wife and she is chaste	10, eng
I must suspect what you say, for her sweet sake.	11, eng

In anger

Huh!

FA HAI   Young scholar Syu, I can see that you are hopelessly in love with her, and so it is useless for me to speak any further. But at Dragonboat Festival time, you should ask her to drink a few cups of yellow wine, and then you will see her turn into her true self, and you will know that I have not been lying to you.

You will not take my advice,   7, in
watch her change with your own eyes.   7, ing

Until we meet again.

SYU   Master, please take care of yourself.

FA HAI *exits*

BLUE   *from inside*
Master, my Lady is asking for you.

SYU   *surprised*
Oh, yes . . .

SYU *wavers in doubt. Then he remembers his love for Lady* WHITE, *and decides that what* FA HAI *said was absurd. He laughs his doubts away*

It is all a lie! *He exits with fruit basket*

SCENE 5   *The Wine Incident*

In the vestibule that leads to the bedroom. BLUE *appears quietly*

BLUE   These weeds and corn stalks will be   7, an
to honor one who could see.   7, an

Though Lords ignore good advice,   7, in
fair is fair and free is free.   7, an

Time flies like an arrow, and here it is the fifth day of the fifth
month, and Dragonboat Festival time again. Although I told my
Sister to stay away from her husband on this day, so he would
not begin to doubt her, she claims that they can never be away
from one another. So right now she is lying in bed, pretending
to be ill, and she told me to go off by myself into the mountains
at high noon. I should have gone by now, but I am worried for
her sake . . .

It's festival time all over the land,   10, ang

Sound of gongs, drums, and firecrackers

And there is no one now to understand.   10, ang
I should have gone to the mountain.   8, ang

WHITE *offstage*
Blue!

BLUE She calls me to be near at hand.   8, ang

Perhaps my dear Sister has decided to leave also?

BLUE *exits* SYU SYAN *appears with a jug of wine. He is slightly
drunk*

SYU I will sing the holidays,   7, ang
and my Lady's gracious ways.   7, ang

My Lady, are you up?

WHITE Yes, I am up.

WHITE *appears upstage left, with* BLUE *on her arm*

I feel weak but I will stand   7, ang
so I can greet my husband.   7, ang

Have you had anything to eat, my dear?

SYU   Yes. While I was in the herb shop just now, I had a few drinks with the other workers to help celebrate the festival. You and I always eat together at the same table, without any change. But unfortunately you are not feeling well today, and I am very concerned. The other workers all told me to cheer you up with a drink, and so here I am. Come on, let's drink. *He empties the cup and refills it*

WHITE   I am not feeling well, and so I cannot have any wine to drink. Dear husband, why don't you go back and thank them for me, and have a drink for me?

SYU   You are always good at drinking, and today is such a nice occasion, we cannot let it pass without having a little wine.

BLUE   *instinctively*
        Today is not like any other day, so please, young Master, do not make my Lady drink.

SYU   *surprised*
        Why is it that our Lady cannot drink today?

BLUE   *covering her mistake*
        I meant, our Lady is not feeling well today. Besides, she is going to have a baby.

SYU   That is true. But still the day is young, and I see no harm in having a few cups of light wine. Oh yes – *To Blue* Blue, you have worked so hard, why don't you have a cup too?

BLUE   Thank you young Master, but you know I never drink.

SYU   All right, you may go take a rest.

BLUE   I'd like to stay with my Lady.

SYU   I will take care of the Lady, you may leave.

WHITE   Blue, why don't you go.

        WHITE *hints with her eye*

BLUE Lady!

WHITE Go.

> BLUE *leaves reluctantly*

SYU My Lady, it is such a rare occasion today, please take a cup of wine for me.

WHITE *diplomatically*
My health keeps me from drinking, and so please forgive me if I do not take any wine.

SYU You are good at drinking, and if you do not have some wine today, all the other workers will laugh at me – so go ahead!

WHITE Well, I . . . I am really not feeling very well, so I can't drink.

SYU If that is the case, then it is all right. I . . . *He bursts into loud laughter*

WHITE What is the matter?

SYU I suddenly thought of a joke.

WHITE What joke?

SYU *weighing it*
Uh . . . I do not think that I should mention it.

WHITE Should there be anything that a husband and wife cannot mention to each other? Please tell me.

SYU Not long ago, someone said to me that you were a . . .

WHITE I am a *what?*

SYU You are – the incarnation of a snake spirit who has existed for a thousand years. And if you drink the yellow wine, you will turn into your true self.

WHITE *greatly disturbed, trying to remain calm*
What? How could anyone say such nonsense? *She smiles* Now I
see – your trying to get me to drink the wine was some sort of
a test . . .

SYU No, no. That is not so. I never believed such nonsense, and that
is why I told you the story. Now let us not joke any more, and
since you are not feeling well, I will not force you again if you
will only have just one drink.

WHITE *smiling*
But what if I suddenly turn into my true self?

SYU *also smiling*
Oh no, please do not be angry with me, my Lady. We love one
another so very much, and I know that you are not a demon.
Even if you were, even so, I would still love you just as much,
And so what do you say if I go and get that small jade cup?

SYU *exits to get cup*

WHITE *Grateful*
Ah . . .

You told it as a joke, my dear husband,	10, ang
and yet now I understand.	7, ang
At first I only saw our wedding band.	10, ang
But now the end is near at hand.	8, ang
There are no flames of hatred I have fanned.	10, ang
Who wants to spoil the life we planned?	8, ang
I should not drink the wine and	7, ang
change myself at your command,	7, ang
yet I fear your reprimand.	7, ang
The love between us might not stand.	8, ang

SYU *enters with jade cup, and pours the wine*

SYU My dear, just drink this cup.

WHITE Now I feel trapped with this cup in my hand –   10, ang

(and after a thousand years of spiritual practice and attainment –) ah well.

My powers may be strong enough to stand.   10, ang

She drinks the cup

To your health!

SYU That is more like. Come, have another one.

WHITE *uncertain*
Well . . .

SYU So we can drink to our marriage for ever.

WHITE For ever?

SYU Exactly! There will be no more doubts or reservations, we will stay together as we grow old.

WHITE Yes, to your health!

She drinks another cup

SYU *pouring again*
And one more!

WHITE *in pain*
Oh . . . Oh . . . Oh . . . The yellow wine has touched me and I do not feel well.

SYU *concerned*
My sweet, are you all right?

WHITE *in pain*
Yes, I am all right. Blue!

SYU Blue is not here now. Come, let me carry you to bed.

WHITE *tries to smile*
I am not drunk yet, I am not drunk yet . . .

She vomits

SYU SYAN *carries* WHITE *to bed behind screen; she vomits again*

SYU Why did I make my dear wife so drunk, when she was pregnant and slightly ill already? I should go to the herb shop and prepare a potion to sober her.

I should think more beforehand.   7, ang

He exits and re-enters with the potion

It was unfair to demand.   7, ang
She was working so hard and   7, ang
she is now with child, as we planned.   8, ang
I open the screen with my hand.   8, ang

No, wait.

She may be from demon land!   7, ang

The priest Fa Hai told me that she is the incarnation of a snake spirit who has existed for a thousand years. and if she drinks the yellow wine, she will turn into her true self. And if she is drunk with wine right now, and if I open her bed screen with my own hand, I might see something that would scare me to death. What should I do? *He thinks* My wife has been so good to me, and she is as fair as a flower, how could she be a demon? I will not listen to Fa Hai! *He listens* Since my wife is sound asleep, why don't I put this potion on the table? It will not be too late for her to take it when she wakes up. *He puts the potion on the table* My dear, the potion is here. I'm going to go.

He is about to go

FA HAI *offstage*
Syu Syan! Behind that bed screen is the potion that will sober you! Get ready to see your wife as she really is!

SYU Ah!

I can hear old Fa Hai say to me	9, au
White is a demon snake of subtlety –	10, au
I can't wake her just to see!	7, au
Yet my doubts move me so strongly,	8, au
now I will call my wife to me.	8, au

There is a moan behind the screen

Be brave, my dear, I am coming to help you. *He opens the screen, and cries out* Oh, no! *He falls.* BLUE *appears quickly*

BLUE Ah! *She touches* SYU *and speaks to the screen*

Wake up, Sister! Wake up, Sister!

WHITE Oh . . .

BLUE Sister, wake up quickly! You really scared him to death!

WHITE *opens the screen and is shocked to see that* SYU *is lying on the ground. She shakes him. After a long while, she finally starts to cry*

WHITE Oh, my poor husband!

Can I believe what I see?	7, au
He lies here so silently.	7, au
He spilled potion in front of me.	8, au
I close my eyes and cry unceasingly.	10, au

Oh, my dear husband!

BLUE Sister, there is no time to cry. We must think of a way to save our young Master.

WHITE You are right – I will leave him in your hands and I will go to the Holy Mountain and try to take some sacred mushrooms.

BLUE Wait a moment, Sister. What will you do if the Holy Guards see you?

WHITE I must take those sacred mushrooms – even if I have to go
through the Kingdom of Knives or the Ocean of Flames, I will
not worry about the Holy Guards.

Sister, please believe in me –	7, au
I must leave immediately.	7, au
Please watch over him carefully.	8, au
If I get back in time, we	7, au
may revive him speedily.	7, au
If I do not return, please see	8, au
him buried in a field growing free	9, au
with green grass for loyalty,	7, au
and underneath a sapling tree –	8, au
let him lie there. As for me,	7, au
I will fly back and cry endlessly.	9, au

BLUE Sister, our young Master will be all right. Please try to believe
that.

BLUE *takes a sword and hands it to* WHITE. WHITE *goes to the
bed and takes a last long look at* SYU, *then turns to* BLUE *and
curtsies*

WHITE Dear Sister, I leave everything to you.

WHITE *exits hurriedly*

SCENE 6 *Guarding the Mountain*

At the Holy Mountain. CRANE BOY *and* DEER BOY *appear, walking on the side*

CRANE BOY,
DEER BOY
Holy Mountain is so grand –	7, ang
sunset and sound from the still land,	8, ang

the smell of grass in the sand,   7, ang
and the purple cliff near at hand –   8, ang
see where those two peaks meet;   6, wu
white clouds expand   4, ang
by Jau Lin Palace, where tall pine trees stand.   10, ang

CRANE BOY I greet you, Holy Officer.

DEER BOY And I greet you.

CRANE BOY You and I are under the order of the Holy Old Man to guard this mountain so no evil demons come into the garden forest and take the sacred mushrooms. Come, let us walk around the mountain.

DEER BOY Very well.

CRANE BOY My strong sword in my hand,   6, ang
I will guard this holy land   7, ang
from the demon's evil band.   7, ang

They exit, dancing

SCENE 7 *Stealing the Mushrooms*

At the Holy Mountain. WHITE *sings behind the curtain*

WHITE I have come here carefully –   7, an

She appears onstage

kept on crying endlessly.   7, an
Little Blue was right that I   7, yu
drank too much and was too free.   7, an
Now Syu Syan is left with Blue   7, ou

and I must climb rapidly,   7, an
take the sacred mushroom home.   7, in

Ah . . .

Holy Guards in front of me,   7, an
I must retreat from where they stand.   8, ang

DEER BOY *appears with sword in hand and blocks her way*

DEER BOY Demon, you must answer me!   7, an
          Where have you come from and why?   7, yu
          And what do you seek to see?   7, an

WHITE Holy Guard, please hear my plea   7, au
       for I must speak honestly.   7, an
       I am called Su Jen, and I   7, yu
       mastered the soul's mystery,   7, an
       because I missed the life on earth.   8, a
       A man named Syu Syan married me   8, an
       and now he lies gravely ill.   7, ing
       He needs mushroms to be free.   7, an

DEER BOY Sacred mushrooms are holy,   7, an
          No one takes them easily.   7, an

WHITE Buddhas are great patient souls,   7, ung
       who have endless charity.   7, an

DEER BOY Do not use your treachery,   7, an
          or my sword swings strong and free!   7, an

WHITE Please give these mushrooms to me,   7, au
       or I will die endlessly.   7, an

DEER BOY You must leave right now or die.   7, yu

He swings sword at WHITE; *she brushes it aside*

WHITE You will have to pardon me.   7, an

WHITE *fights with the* DEER BOY; *she wounds him, takes some of the sacred mushrooms, and is about to leave. The* CRANE BOY *hears the commotion and appears. With the mushrooms in her mouth,* WHITE *fights both the* DEER *and* CRANE BOYS *strenuously. She fails to beat them and falls down on the ground, but she still keeps the mushrooms held tightly in her mouth. The* CRANE BOY *raises his sword over her*

CRANE BOY She demon, you are about to die!

The HOLY OLD MAN *from the South appears hurriedly with the* HOLY BOY

HOLY
OLD MAN Stop, Crane Boy! *To* WHITE So, Su Jen White, what nerve you have to come to Holy Mountain and take the sacred mushrooms!

WHITE Oh, Holy Old Man, I do not care about my life, but my poor husband is about to die!

HOLY
OLD MAN Su Jen White, because of your devotion, and because you are about to bear a child, I will let you live. Take the sacred mushrooms with you and go home to save your husband's life. You may leave.

WHITE *cries out with joy at this news*

WHITE Oh, thank you, Holy Old Man!

Taking these mushrooms with me,	7, an
I will go home immediately!	8, an
Thank you for your charity.	7, an
Now my husband will be free.	7, an

She exits

DEER BOY Huh!

HOLY
OLD MAN Do not stand in her way!

HOLY OLD MAN *looks after* WHITE, *then he sighs with disapproval*

Holy Boys!

BOYS   Yes.

HOLY
OLD MAN   Let's go back to Holy Mountain.

All exit together

SCENE 8   *Driving Out the Doubts*

In the bedroom

WHITE   I brought the sacred mushrooms back with me   10, an
to save my husband's life, yet now that he   10, an
is well again, he is unkind to me.   10, an
It hurts my heart, and I cry secretly.   10, an

BLUE *appears angrily*

BLUE   Syu Syan does not take care of his dear wife,   10, en
and makes his bookkeeping a place to hide.   10, ing

Sister, have you made yourself up?

WHITE   *happily*
Oh, Sister Blue, you are back!

BLUE   Huh! Our Scholar Syu! As soon as he saw me coming, he went
to work on his bookkeeping, and made a big noise with his
abacus. But when I took a closer look, I saw it was the accounts
from months and months ago!

WHITE   *sadly*
I suppose he still doesn't want to speak to me . . .

BLUE Yes, that is true! Here you went through all sorts of trouble, you escaped death many times for his sake, and finally you saved his life. And now he turns around and treats you coldly and without kindness. If you ask me, you should leave him and go somewhere as far away from here as possible, so you won't have to suffer so much.

WHITE But don't you know I am already pregnant?

BLUE Of course I know. Well, after you give birth, just give the child to Scholar Syu. What else is there to do?

WHITE Sister Blue, Syu Syan and I love each other so much, the sea may go dry and the rocks may rot, but we will never let ourselves be separated.

Little Sister, you give me your advice,	10, in
You say that I should go away, so my heart will	
not break.	14, eng
But I love Syu Syan, and I always will!	10, ing
The sky may turn black, the earth may grow old, but	
I am still his wife!	16, en

BLUE Sister,

we two were never used to sitting still,	10, ing
how could we live a life of sacrifice?	10, in
What we must fear is Syu Syan's ill will.	9, ing
You cannot live with this man, so follow my advice.	13, in
You must leave him, and pay the painful price,	10, in
before love changes to hate and hearts to ice.	11, in

WHITE From what I have seen, that will never happen.

Your will is strong and you speak with great skill,	10, ing
but one must go slow in matters of the will.	11, ing

BLUE Well, since we are not going to go, then you must think of how to do away with all his doubts.

WHITE You are right.

What will ensure that he must love me still?   10, ing

I have it!

This fine seven-foot silver satin will!   10, ing

Dear Sister, I have thought of something.

BLUE What is it, Sister?

WHITE I will take this white satin on my waist and turn it into a silver snake, and make it coil around the beam on the ceiling in the kitchen. Then we will say that a snake has appeared here and tell my husband to come and take a look. When he sees the snake with us, I am sure he will not have any doubts any more.

BLUE That is excellent! Now Sister, you arrange it while I go and bring our Master here. *Exits hurriedly*

WHITE This is it:
'When mirrors are dim, the hand   7, ang
dusts them with a silver strand.'   7, ang

BLUE *appears*

BLUE Mr Dou has pushed our Scholar Syu in here.

DOU *offstage*
Master, the Lady has been waiting for a long while, so go in quickly.

DOU *appears, pushing* SYU SYAN. WHITE *rises to greet him*

WHITE Dear husband!

SYU *is scared and behaves awkwardly*

SYU My Lady. *He sits reluctantly*

WHITE Blue told me you were doing some bookkeeping in the store. Now that you have just got well, you should not work so hard.

SYU I am all right, I am all right.

WHITE I cannot get over my worries, so I asked Blue to prepare some dishes to go with our wine.

SYU I do not think I care to drink.

WHITE But you must. Blue, go and get the wine.

BLUE Yes. *Exits*

WHITE Dear husband,
Since Dragonboat Festival, you have been cold.   11, yi
Will you still love me when we are both old?   10, yi

BLUE *screams offstage*
My Lady, hurry in here, my Lady, hurry!!

WHITE Oh, what is it? *To* SYU SYAN My dear, please wait for me. I will be right back. *Exits gracefully*

SYU Ah!
She is so fair – her lips, her hair, her brows.   10, ei
A shame these demons cannot keep their vows.   10, ei

WHITE *hurries onstage, expression of shock*

SYU Why are you frightened?

WHITE Blue went into the kitchen a moment ago to get the wine, and she saw a silver snake coiled around the ceiling beam!

SYU *trembles*
What – a silver snake again!

BLUE *appears*

BLUE   Young Master and my Lady, do not be alarmed. Mr Dou told me the snake is only a creature that protects the house. It will not hurt anyone.

SYU   What? It is only a creature that protects the house, and it will not hurt anyone?

BLUE   Yes. Only when 'men are aware and women are watchful' will this silver snake appear. It is an omen of good luck to our house.

WHITE   Oh? It is an omen of good luck to our house?

SYU   Has the snake left?

BLUE   No. It is still there. Let us go and look at it.

SYU   Is it all right to take a look?

BLUE   Of course it is all right. I am not afraid at all.

SYU   If that is the case, let us go and see.

SYU, BAI, *and* BLUE *exit from right; then they reappear*

SYU   Ha, ha! This is perfect.

The snake is a good sign for humankind,   10, yun
and so I throw all doubt clear out of mind.   10, yun

And this snake is a good sign for us! Oh my Lady, this reminds me of something I have been thinking about.

WHITE   What is that?

SYU   On the day of the Dragonboat Festival, when you got drunk, and I went to get some potion to give you, when I opened the screen of your bed, I swear there was a snake that looked exactly like this one.

WHITE What? On the day of the Dragonboat Festival, you saw it also?

SYU Yes, I think this was it. And my illness came from it.

BLUE But why didn't you say so earlier?

SYU Uh . . . I must have lost my head, thinking that some stranger's words were true. How ridiculous! My Lady, please sit down. *They sit* Get the large cups, Blue. I shall have a few drinks with my Lady, to ask her pardon for the way I have been behaving over this past half month.

WHITE My dear, you have just gotten well. Perhaps you had better not drink.

SYU It's all right. I understand everything now, so the illness is also all over.

WHITE On the day of the Dragonboat Festival, because I was ill, I did not drink very much with you. I might as well make it up to-night. But because we have both just got well, could we use little cups?

SYU Whatever you say.

WHITE Blue, move all the cups and dishes into the bedroom. *To* SYU Let me get the lantern.

SYU Thank you.

WHITE Dear husband!

This month has been hard for your wife.   8, en

SYU Now our hearts are filled with good will.   8, ing

WHITE Dear husband,

do not listen to bad advice.   8, in

SYU Dear Lady,

He points to twin stars in the sky

like those stars, we swear love still.   7, ing

SYU SYAN *and* WHITE *exit, hand in hand.* BLUE, *very pleased, follows*

SCENE 9 *Going to the Mountain*

Near the river. FA HAI, *holding a stick, appears alone onstage*

FA HAI I hold my stick in my hand,   7, ang
   and wait for the lost husband.   7, ang

He sees SYU *coming, steps aside, and hides himself*

SYU One thing I do not understand.   8, ang
  Festival time, at my command,   8, ang
  my wife White got drunk in bed and   8, ang
  I brought her potion in my hand.   8, ang
  Before her screen I paused to stand   8, ang
  and I could feel my fears expand!   8, ang
  Was my wife from some demon land?   8, ang
  I know the snake's supposed to stand   8, ang
  for luck, but if luck was at hand,   8, ang
  was our place the right place to land?   8, ang
  Now I think these things by river sand.   9, ang

Ah! How beautiful the Yangtze River is!

The Yangtze is grand, truly grand.   7, ang

FA HAI *advances quietly*

FA HAI   So long as you admire the mighty Yangtze, why don't you come visit at Golden Mountain?

SYU   Ah, Master! You are here. I have not seen you for a long time.

FA HAI   I am an old man, and I have not been feeling well, in fact I almost died.

SYU   What was the matter?

FA HAI   I had a bad shock, and I became very ill.

SYU   Old Master, with your quick and subtle wit, are you still able to be shocked?

FA HAI   It happened so fast how could I keep from being shocked?

SYU   What a coincidence! I also experienced the very same thing.

FA HAI   What? You mean you also had a bad shock? Don't tell me you had some wine potion?

SYU   *surprised*
What – yes, that is precisely right.

FA HAI   Did what I say come true?

SYU   It came true all right, but then the snake also appeared coiled on the beam of the kitchen ceiling. And my wife said: 'This is a good snake. It will not harm anyone.'

FA HAI   There is more to it than that. That day, you had a bad shock and died. Bai Su Jen went to the Holy Mountain where she stole the sacred mushrooms and saved your life. The 'snake' that was coiled on the beam of the kitchen ceiling was a piece of silver satin which she made to look like a snake by means of her sorcery. If your wife were not a demon, how could she do a thing like that?

syu But if my wife went to the Holy Mountain and stole the sacred mushrooms to save my life – then she would have to be a very good person.

FA HAI The only reason that she saved your life is that she loves your handsome face, and so she allows you to go on living a little longer.

syu But she is seven months pregnant – don't tell me that is also some of her sorcery.

FA HAI Dear friend, please listen:

A man goes to Temple and	7, an
meets a fair maid near at hand.	7, ang
Her stepmother rules her then,	7, en
makes her heed every command.	7, ang
This man sees her, loves her too,	7, ou
and he becomes her husband.	7, ang
Later she has a boy child.	7, dz
They live well, as they had planned.	7, ang

Now FA HAI *tries to scare* syu

One night the wife, growing bold,	7, yi
turns into a white serpent and	8, ang
devours her child greedily,	7, au
and then she kills her husband.	7, ang
You are young and fair and you	7, ou
are now the white snake's husband.	7, ang
When your charms all disappear,	7, ai

– young man, oh, my young man –

you will die – and by her hand!   7, ang

syu *is frightened*

syu Ah, Master! Is there any way to save myself?

FA HAI   Become a Buddhist, and you will save yourself.

SYU   I promised that I would become a Buddhist when I was ill. To-day, with my wife's knowledge, I was going to go to Temple and burn incense to keep my promise. But I need some guidance from you.

FA HAI   My advice is not given for nothing.

SYU   Here are ten ounces of silver, I hope my Master will take it.

FA HAI   Some say that enlightenment is not bought with money.

SYU   What do you say?

FA HAI   Join my monastery.

SYU   Well . . . Can I do it tomorrow?

FA HAI   Tomorrow will be too late.

SYU   Isn't my Master in too much of a hurry?

FA HAI   One can't be in too much of a hurry to save someone from damnation.

SYU   If that is so, then please receive me. *He bows*

FA HAI   Buddha Amitabha! Follow your Master! Ha ha ha . . .

> FA HAI *takes* SYU *by the arm, ready to leave.* SYU *hesitates and turns back*

FA HAI   Syu Syan! Where are you going?

SYU   Would it be all right if I went home and thought about it for awhile?

FA HAI   Haven't you heard: 'It is easy to convert, but hard to turn back.'

SYU   I do not want to be converted any more.

FA HAI   What is there left for you at home to hold on to?

SYU   I do not care for my house, but I do care for my wife's love.

FA HAI   You see – your earthly desires are not yet broken. You want to know how you can avoid catastrophe? Well, you told me you were going to go to the Golden Mountain Temple to burn incense and keep your promise?

SYU   That is right.

FA HAI   After you have done that, this old priest will explain to you in detail all of the secret reasons behind everything. Then you yourself can choose between death and life and between happiness and misery.

SYU   That is good.

FA HAI   Go.

SYU   I am going. This is the way it is: 'One admires being married, but one also admires being one with the gods.' I, Syu Syan, am in two boats at the same time.

FA HAI   This swift sword I keep with me   7, an
cuts clean and will set you free.   7, an

Ha ha ha! Let us go, Syu Syan. Amitabha!

He takes SYU *by the arm, triumphant. They exit*

SCENE 10   *Crossing the River*

At the Yangtze River. WHITE *and* BLUE *appear onstage rowing a boat*

WHITE   We came by boat swiftly.   6, au
Sister Blue?

BLUE   Yes, Sister.

WHITE I have been thinking about the day my husband and I met by the lake, and later on how much he loved me and how much I worship him. Yet now that he has believed old Fa Hai's words so easily, I have been cast aside quite casually. I cannot help feeling sad and bitter.

BLUE   Dear Sister, the way things are, it is useless to feel sad and bitter. The important thing is to hurry to the Golden Mountain Temple and come face to face with old Fa Hai.

WHITE Let's go.

We ride the waves of the Yangtze,   8, au
to see the balding donkey   7, au
who stole Syu from his family.   8, au
Three days Syu has not seen me.   7, au
In that place he is not free.   7, au
I hate that holy place so fiercely!   9, au

Sister Blue,

Our oars and swords are both ready   8, au
as we row across the sea.   7, au
We will kill that old donkey!   7, au

SCENE 11 *Lady White Demands Her Husband*

At Golden Mountain

FA HAI *sings offstage*
A moment ago, I prayed deeply.   9, an

FA HAI *can now be seen standing on the cliff outside the Gate of Golden Mountain Temple*

Syu learns Buddhist truth from me.   7, an
Those demons are coming, I see.   8, an
I'll answer each inquiry.   7, an

BLUE   You bald-headed donkey! Give our young Master back!

WHITE   *quickly*
Blue, do not speak like that. *She begs* FA HAI *patiently* Old
Master, three days ago my husband Syu Syan came here to burn
incense in your Temple. Would you please go inside and ask
him to come out, so we can go home together.

FA HAI Who is your husband?

WHITE   Syu Syan.

FA HAI Syu Syan is not in our temple. You must look for him elsewhere.

WHITE   Before my husband left home, he said very clearly he was coming to this temple to burn incense and keep some promise that
he made. He and I love each other dearly. we are inseparable.
Please, Old Master, let him come out so we can join each other.

FA HAI I may as well tell you the truth: your husband has become a
monk by my guidance and advice, and so it is impossible for him
to go home now.

WHITE   How can this be? He and I had sworn to love each other until
death. If he is taken away from me like this, I know no way to
ease my mind. You are a priest and well esteemed, and so you
ought to let my husband go home with me. That way you will
show yourself to be a true Buddhist, and that way my husband
and I will always be grateful to you for your virtue and kindness.
Oh, Old Master –

That Scholar Syu and I go hand in hand,   10, ang
like lovers who are known through all the land.   10, ang
If you would only give me back my husband,   11, ang
our deep gratitude to you would always stand.   11, ang

FA HAI You bitch.

BLUE *is furious but stops before making a move*

Once Syu was so holy, this poor husband –   10, ang
How can his vows to the white snake still stand?   10, ang
You should go back to your O-mei homeland,   10, ang
or I will kill you both with my own hand.   10, ang

BLUE Listen, you bald-headed donkey!

My Lady was in love with her husband,   10, ang
and you are spoiling everything they planned.   10, ang
Give Syu Syan back to us as we command,   10, ang
or we will flood your place with Yangtze sand!   10, ang

WHITE Little Blue, stop talking nonsense. My dear Old Master!

Blue is so rude, she does not understand,   10, ang
Not like your noble soul which is so grand.   10, ang
Buddha treats each creature with equal hand,   10, ang
that is why humans praise his kind command.   10, ang

I, Su Jen White

live by the river with my dear husband.   10, ang
I am about to have a baby and   10, ang
I beg you, Holy Master, understand,   10, ang
and let me take my husband to our land.   10, ang

FA HAI Su Jen White, I must ignore your demand.   10, ang
I tell you, you cannot have your husband.   10, ang
Holy priests cannot let these demons stand,   10, ang
this is the Buddha's most solemn command.   10, ang

WHITE *suppresses her anger*

WHITE Thousands of sick have been healed by my hand,   10, ang
Lady White is well known throughout the land.   10, ang

You speak of demons – you should understand,	10, ang
since you came between me and my husband.	10, ang

FA HAI *suppresses his temper*

FA HAI	I have a dragon stick here in my hand,	10, ang
	and it will not let evil demons stand.	10, ang

WHITE	You have a dragon stick there in your hand,	10, ang
	but I have truth, which all men understand.	10, ang

BLUE *can no longer hold her anger*

BLUE	Do not speak, this man will not understand!	10, ang
	We will wreck his temple; it will not stand!	10, ang

FA HAI	Holy Guard, come in here as I command	10, ang

HOLY
GUARDS *offstage*
Yes, Master! *They appear*

FA HAI	Seize those two demons – chase them in a band!	10, ang

WHITE *and* BLUE *exit hurriedly*

HOLY
GUARDS Yes, Master! *They exit, chasing the two women*

SCENE 12   *The Water Battle*

At Golden Mountain Temple: The Yangtze River flows angrily. With bitterness and anger, WHITE *appears with a battle flag. After a few moments, she throws the flag to* BLUE. BLUE *takes the flag and starts to call all the water animals.* WHITE *reappears among the water animals and calls to them*

WHITE Listen to me:

De – de – depend on me,   6, au
De – de – depend on me,   repeat
We – we – we lived together so happily.   11, au
Then – then – then Fai Hai came by so cunningly.   11, au
A – a – asking my husband to force wine on me.   12, au
Syu – Syu – Syu needed sacred mushrooms to be free.   12, au
But – but – but he listened to Fa Hai instead of me!   13, au
And – and – and then he discarded me so easily!   13, au
The – the – the cause of all of this is the old bald-
      headed donkey!   16, au
My – my – my hatred is as deep as the sea!   11, au

Brothers and Sisters, let us go and destroy Old Fa Hai!

WATER
ANIMALS Yes!

The HOLY GUARDS *appear, and the* WATER ANIMALS *advance to fight them.* WHITE *and* BLUE *also fight. They are winning at first, but then* WHITE *feels the pain of the baby.* BLUE *and the others protect her, and they slowly retreat.* WHITE *cries out bitterly*

WHITE My husband!

She exits with her followers while the HOLY GUARDS *keep right behind them*

SCENE 13 *Escaping from the Mountain*

In the Buddhist's Hall. SYU SYAN *appears with book of Sutra in his hand*

SYU I came to this place so I could be free,   10, an
but now the days go by so endlessly.   10, an
I wish my dear wife were close to me.   9, an

Sound of drums is heard

Ah!

I wonder what all that noise can be?   9, an

A novice monk appears with cup of tea

SYU   Brother, please tell me, what are those voices outside the Mountain Gate?

NOVICE   Hm, I cannot tell you that.

SYU   *realizing*
         Don't tell me my wife is here looking for me.

NOVICE   Well, you guessed it. It *is* your wife who has come looking for you. She is so pretty! But that maid of hers, how fierce she is!

SYU   Where are they now? Let me go see my wife.

NOVICE   Don't go. How could you be allowed to see her at a time like this? Besides, the Old Master says that your wife is a demon, and that she is inhuman.

SYU   Her feelings for me are very human. Now I know what must be going on: all that yelling that comes from outside the Mountain Gate, it means that the Master is fighting with my wife.

NOVICE   The Master sent for the Holy Guards to catch your wife. Now they are fighting violently.

Sound of drums again

FA HAI *yells from offstage*

FA HAI   Guards, do not let Su Jen White escape. Surround her!

Another sound of drums

SYU *worried*

Oh no! My wife is seven months pregnant, and how, how, how can she take all this violent fighting? Brother, please, let me go out!

NOVICE What are you going out for?

SYU I – I – I want to help . . .

NOVICE Help whom?

SYU My wife.

NOVICE You just want to make trouble for me. The Old Master has magic powers, and I think your wife is going to be caught at any moment.

SYU Oh no!

Heavy drums

WHITE *offstage*
Where are you, Syu? Where are you, Syu? Syu!

SYU Here I am, my Lady!

To Novice

Dear little Brother!

Little Brother, please give me a hand,	9, ang
she is calling for her husband!	8, ang

Little Brother, hurry and help me out of here and I promise I will reward you.

NOVICE Wait a moment – you can hear the yelling as it gets further and further away, mostly likely your wife has escaped.

SYU Then I must hurry over. If little Brother will let me . . . Please, don't you see, I am kneeling to you . . .

NOVICE All right, all right, don't get so excited. So long as the Master has not come back yet, I may as well let you try to run for it . . .

SYU Thank you, thank you little Brother!

NOVICE Follow me! There is a little trail over here. So long as no one knows, you had better hurry.

SYU That's fine. My Brother leads me by the hand.   8, ang

They are about to exit, when FA HAI *appears*

FA HAI Are you breaking my command?   7, ang

NOVICE Master, he . . . he . . . he wanted me to take him to see you. He said he wants to beg forgiveness for his – his – his wife.

FA HAI Hmm! It seems as if his mind is still with humankind. How can he ever become a monk?

SYU *is silent, his head is bent low*

FA HAI All right, Syu Syan. I defeated Su Jen White but she escaped to Lin An. The mansion of Chyou has been burned down to the ground, so this evil demon has no place to go. If she does go elsewhere, she will certainly stir up more trouble. So listen to me. This is what I will do: I will give you a Wind God, and I will let you go and live with demon White for one month. Where is the Wind God?

WIND GOD *appears*

WIND GOD Here I am.

FA HAI Quickly, take Syu Syan to Lin An.

WIND GOD Yes, Master.

> WIND GOD *covers* SYU, *and they exit*

SCENE 14 *The Broken Bridge*

> *Near West Lake.* WHITE, *looking poor and disreputable, appears*

WHITE Flying from the fight, I rage on my way!   10, wo

My heartless husband!

> BLUE *catches up with* WHITE. *They come together and cry*

Fa Hai caused chaos here today,   8, wo
and made Master Syu betray   7, wo
his wife to my great dismay.   7, wo

> *She falls down.* BLUE *helps her up*

BLUE Sister, what is it?

WHITE I feel a pain inside, and I cannot take another step. What shall I do?

BLUE I think your baby is on its way. Let us go to the bridge ahead and sit for awhile. Maybe then we can think of what we should do.

WHITE Since things are as they are, I really have no choice.

> BLUE *helps to carry* WHITE, *as they look at the lake*

WHITE *solemnly*
Sister Blue, isn't this the Broken Bridge?

BLUE   That's right.

WHITE   Oh, Broken Bridge! I remember when I first met Syu in the rain, I was also passing by this bridge. Now the bridge has not broken, but my heart has shattered in pieces!

As in old times, West Lake is near at hand –	10, ang
The eye sees, but the heart does not live in this land.	12, ang
Syu does not remember the things we planned.	10, ang
I bite my lips and cry for my husband.	10, ang

BLUE   Such a heartless man! I told you many times to give him up, and you would not listen to me. Now here you are, wandering around, homeless and pregnant. If I see Syu Syan again, I will not let him go so easily.

WHITE   I too am angry at Syu Syan for his heartlessness and disregard. But when I think it all over, I can only blame old Fa Hai for interfering and making things the way they are.

BLUE   Although it was all the fault of old Fa Hai, still, Syu Syan should not have forgotten your feelings for him, when he listened to Fa Hai.

WHITE   I can understand how Syu Syan may have doubted me. I still say it was all the fault of old Fa Hai.

BLUE   My! Even now you take your husband's side. Haven't you had enough of him?

WHITE   Dear Sister Blue,

He and I swore our love eternally.	10, an
Man and wife should trust each other freely.	10, an

BLUE
Sister, you stay the same. You do not see	10, an
that Syu Syan is not the way he used to be.	11, an

Enraged, she unsheathes her sword

I will kill anyone who dares betray!	10, in

SYU *shouts offstage*
Hurry, Hurry!

SYU SYAN *hurries onstage*

SYU The Holy Wind carried me,   7, an
thinking of love continually.   8, an

He sees WHITE *and* BLUE, *and is filled with surprise and joy*

Ah!

Oh she is like a withered willow tree!   10, an
And Blue has drawn a sword for me,   8, an
how she rages endlessly!   7, an
I understand their hating me,   8, an
for I have caused them such agony.   9, an
I don't care what happens to me.   8, an

My Lady!

WHITE *surprised, cries out*
Dear husband!

BLUE Syu Syan, you have come at the right time!

She starts to attack SYU *with her sword, he runs away and* BLUE *pursues him. Both exit*

WHITE Blue! *She runs after them, staggering* Blue! *She exits.* SYU *reappears, still running*

SYU I'm scared to death at what I see!   8, an

BLUE *reappears*

BLUE Where do you think you're going? *She continues chasing* SYU; *they run around the stage*

WHITE *running behind them*
Blue, stop that! Blue, stop that!

BLUE *waves her sword;* SYU *kneels before* WHITE

SYU My Lady, please save me, please save me!

WHITE *protects* SYU *from* BLUE's *sword. She is filled with sadness and anger*

WHITE You, you, you have come to this – you ask me to save you? you, you, you . . .

You made me feel ill and	6, ang
you made me drink herb wine and	7, ang
you deceived my soul and	6, ang
you swore you gave me your hand,	7, an
you kept Fa Hai's command.	7, ang
You hurt me, my dear husband,	7, ang
and after all we had planned,	7, ang
and I am pregnant, I do not understand!	11, ang
You look on and were so bland	7, ang
while I fought Holy Guards hand to hand.	9, ang
The fight was fierce, my poor head aches, I hurt inside,	
I can barely stand.	17, ang
But you stayed safe, as if unmanned.	8, ang
Now I feel your heart. Touch with your hand.	8, ang
How dare you face me now, husband?	8, ang

SYU My Lady,

I heard the fighting outside, and	8, ang
I was crying for you, and	7, ang
I tried to lend a helping hand –	8, an
but Fa Hai had made his command.	8, ang

BLUE Since Fa Hai would not allow you to come to see my Lady, then how were you able to travel thousands of miles from Jen Jyang to this place?

SYU Well, that is because . . .

BLUE *interrupting*
Did Fa Hai send you here to get my Sister and me? You are such
a heartless person, I am going to kill you and be done with it!

SYU No, no, no such thing! Please listen to me. Please listen!

WHITE *to* BLUE
Let us hear what he has to say.

BLUE *points at* SYU *angrily*
Talk!

SYU My Lady, and Sister Blue,

There on the bank of the Yangtze,	8, an
Master Fa Hai advised me.	7, an
I wanted to go home quickly	8, an
but, kept in the monastery,	8, an
I thought of your love endlessly.	8, an

Dear wife,

How could I sleep, not being free?	8, an
Then you came searching for me.	7, an
I heard, but I could not see.	7, an
You and Fa Hai fought fiercely,	7, an
I knew, and it wounded me.	7, an
One monk there helped me, he	6, an
released me so I could flee.	7, an
But Ta Hai came after me.	7, an
The winds blew me home easily.	8, an
Now that you are here, I see,	7, an
I could die now happily.	7, an

BLUE Bah!

You say you missed your Lady,	7, an
why did you doubt so readily?	8, an

When my Lady fought so fiercely,   8, an
why did you side with the Old Donkey?   9, an
Fa Hai must have set you free   7, an
to spy on your family!   7, an
Your fine words aren't fooling me!   7, an
Bad man, prepare to meet your enemy!   10, an

BLUE *raises her sword and is about to kill* SYU. WHITE *stops her hurriedly*

WHITE Sister Blue!

You should handle your sword more cautiously.   10, an

To SYU

My loved and hated one!

Dear Syu, put by your fear and hear me.   9, an
I am not merely human – I   8, yu
also have a snake spirit in me.   9, an

Hearing that WHITE *is telling the truth,* BLUE *is anxious to stop her, but* WHITE *ignores her*

Seeking love and family   7, a
I came to West Lake softly,   7, an
saw you, and you spoke to me.   7, an
I loved how you felt all things very deeply,   11, an
like your sweet mother's memory,   8, an
and how you refused the slightest charity.   11, an
We lived and loved so dearly,   7, an
who could have known our destiny?   8, an
We stayed in Jen Hyang, where we   7, an
worked in an herb shop patiently.   8, an
You became ill with an injury   9, an
and I had to save your life: it was up to me.   12, an
We're not alike, yet I treated you kindly   11, an
and am about to bear you a baby.   10, an
Oh you should not have turned on me!   8, an

You joined Fa Hai's company.   7, an
I wanted you right here with me;   8, an
each night I waited for you hopefully,   10, an
my pillow wet with tears – alas, poor me,   10, an
and my dreams were filled with thoughts of you – ah me.   11, an
I went to Temple recklessly   8, an
just to get you back with me.   7, an
If Blue had not fought so fiercely,   8, an
I fear I might well have lost our baby.   10, an
Blue thinks you are our enemy.   8, an

Oh, my loved and hated one!

Now you should face yourself in all honesty.   11, an

BLUE *to* SYU
  All right, Syu Syan, my Lady has told you the whole truth, so
  now you can go back and join your real Master, Fa Hai. *To*
  WHITE Sister, let's go.

WHITE Sister, listen to what he has to say.

SYU My Lady has spoken truly.   8, an
     I remember all past things very clearly.   11, an
     We met when it was rainy,   7, an
     we loved, and we worked patiently.   8, an
     I made you get drunk so thoughtlessly,   9, an
     and when I stood there in front of your bed it
             frightened me.   14, an
     You went to get some herbs to set me free.   10, an
     You saved me by your bravery,   8, an
     I went to the monastery,   8, an
     and Fa Hai tried to convert me.   8, an
     I stayed there and I could not flee.   8, an
     I am sorry you were waiting endlessly,   11, an
     you had to come in search of me.   8, an
     even with child you came in search of me.   10, an
     Then I saw your heart was good and you loved me truly. 13, an
     Then I saw that you suffered thousands of times for me. 13, an

Oh, my Lady,

Demon or not, I love you eternally.   11, an

BLUE *comes forward and grabs* SYU SYAN

BLUE Syu Syan!

I love the honey sugar way you lie!   10, yu

You traitor! You only know how to make sure of your own comfort. Since when have you ever cared about my Lady's suffering?

WHITE Blue, now he knows.

BLUE How do you know that he knows? *Pushes* SYU SYAN *away*
Dear Sister,

You are too kind to this absurdity,   10, an
he will go on changing his mind endlessly.   11, an

SYU My Lady, Sister Blue,

If you see a change in me,   7, an
cut me up mercilessly.   7, an

WHITE Oh no!

WHITE *helps* SYU *stand up, embraces him and cries*

BLUE *sighs and sings*
They are still deeply in love, I see,   9, an
so they will have to suffer endlessly.   10, an
I think I'd better leave and let them be.   10, an

She curtsies sadly

Sister, please take good care of yourself. I am saying goodbye to you.

WHITE *stops her quickly*
      Sister Blue!

      We went through so much, how could you leave me?   10, an
      You know I am going to have a baby.   10, au
      And should I be alone and lonely?   9, an
      To leave me now would be such cruelty.   10, an

      Sister Blue . . . WHITE *begins to cry*

BLUE Sister, control yourself.

      We will be together eternally,   10, an
      before we came we vowed our love, and we   10, an
      remained together through adversity.   10, an
      I hope you give birth to a good baby,   10, an

      I hope that Syu . . .

      WHITE *cries. Ashamed,* SYU SYAN *lowers his head*

      I hope that Syu can love you endlessly.   10, an
      If he indulges in hypocrisy,   10, an
      this sword will cut him up quite easily.   10, an

SYU Sister Blue!

      Gold is tested constantly.   7, an
      I know I love my Lady.   7, an
      Blue, please do believe in me,   7, an
      try to trust my loyalty.   7, an

WHITE Dear husband, where shall we settle down?

SYU Why don't we go to the house of my Sister's husband?

WHITE All right, but please do not mention what happened at Golden
      Mountain.

SYU Of course not.

WHITE   Come, Sister Blue!

> Once again we've become a family,   10, an
> We will nest like swallows in a tall tree.   10, an
> Let's go to Ching Pwo Gate, Blue, please help me.   10, an

WHITE *turns and looks back at the lake*

> Oh, West Lake – you still seem just the same to me!   11, an

All exit left

SCENE 15   *The Joining of the Bowl*

> *Interior of the Lin An residence.* SYU SYAN's *older* SISTER *appears with some colorful baby clothing*

SISTER   How nice!

> From now on, a new Syu child comes to stay.   10, wo
> I'll dress the baby in a charming way.   10, wo

BLUE *appears with baby in her arms*

BLUE   Such a joy for my Sister to give birth.   10, e
        It makes up for her sufferings on earth.   10, e

        Oh, dear Aunt, here you are!

SISTER   Good morning, Blue. Is my sister-in-law up?

BLUE   Yes, she has been up for a long time.

SISTER   Where is my brother?

BLUE   The young Master is out picking flowers. He said that he is going to dress my Lady up.

SISTER Today is the day that my sister-in-law has had her baby for one full month, and so she deserves to be dressed up. Here are the baby clothes I got last night. Also here are a gold chain and a bib and a pair of little socks – consider these things gifts from his aunt.

BLUE Oh, they are beautiful! My Lady also made a lot of clothes for him. Enough to wear until he is one year old. Let us go and dress the baby now.

SISTER Come along to my room.

Both exit

SYU SYAN *appears with flowers*

SYU My baby now is one month old.   8, yi
     Neighbors will come to behold.   7, yi
     These fresh flowers are like gold.   7, yi
     My love for White must be told.   7, yi

     My dear, are you up from bed? Hurry and come here to get yourself ready. Our friends and relatives will soon be here.

WHITE *speaking offstage*
       I am coming!

SYU Wait a moment, I will come help you.

SYU SYAN *enters the room and helps* WHITE. *She looks tired but happy*

WHITE It feels good to be up and around here.   10, ai
       Now I must care about how I appear.   10, ai
       Dear husband, hold the mirror very near.   10, ai

WHITE *looks into the mirror and* SYU SYAN *combs her hair*

SYU This mirror fills me with so much good cheer. 10, ai
     The beauty of my wife is still so clear,   10, ai

like some good goddess in her own bright sphere.   10, ai
I will fasten a flower by her ear.   10, ai

SYU *puts a flower above her ear,* WHITE *turns her head and smiles at him*

WHITE From now on, there is nothing more to fear.   10, ai

FA HAI *suddenly appears*

FA HAI Syu Syan! Your association with the evil demon Su Jen White is ended right now. I am putting her inside this bowl. And you will follow me to Golden Mountain.

SYU SYAN *quickly covers* WHITE *with his own body*

SYU Ah! You – you – you are here again!

WHITE You old bald-headed donkey!

WHITE *unsheathes her sword and charges.* FA HAI *defends himself with his stick*

FA HAI Where is Wei Two?

WEI TWO *raises the Golden Bowl*

WHITE Blue, Blue!!

WHITE *is confined by the Golden Ray of the Golden Bowl*

FA HAI That Blue of yours has been defeated by me and she is no longer here.

WHITE This is terrible!

He says that Blue is not here.   7, ai

BLUE, *however, appears with her sword, waving and charging, bravely trying to save* WHITE. *She fights first with several* HOLY

GUARDS, *and then with* FA HAI's *dragon stick which* FA HAI *has handed to the* HOLY GUARDS. *She is defeated.*

BLUE   Sister, Sister!

WHITE   Dear Sister, leave immediately so you can avenge my husband and me!

FA HAI   Holy Guards, kill!

BLUE   Thief!

BLUE fights bravely

Sister!

She retreats offstage

WHITE   Ah . . .

We two are separated here.	8, ai
I wish dear Blue would reappear	8, ai
I need her another year!	7, ai

She pulls SYU SYAN *tightly*

Dear husband!

We were in love and our love was sincere,	10, ai
I saved your life because you were so dear;	10, ai
I also fought for you and had no fear;	10, ai
I gave birth to your baby here.	8, ai
Now all this must disappear.	7, ai

Oh my dear husband Syu!

SYU | | |
|---|---|
| My heart is torn apart here. | 7, ai |
| I kneel to Fa Hai in my fear, | 8, ai |
| that he may be kind and clear. | 7, ai |

Dear Master, since my wife has not committed any crime, why then are you so vicious towards her? If she should die, what about the love that has been between us, and who will take care of our one-month-old baby son? Master, I hope that you will open your heart to kindness and understanding, and to show you my devotion, I will kneel down right here in front of you.

FA HAI *turns aside and ignores* SYU

FA HAI Hmm!

WHITE *stops* SYU SYAN, *who is about to kneel down*

WHITE Dear one!

Why talk of love to this butcher here?   9, ai

The baby cries

Now please bring the baby near.   7, ai

SYU SYAN's *sister appears with the baby,* SYU MENG JYAU

Oh, my son! WHITE *takes* MEN JYAU *and sings*

Why is he crying in fear?   7, ai
He has to leave his mother dear.   8, ai
This is the last time I will dry your tear.   10, ai

Darling baby!

Your mother will never reappear   9, ai

She turns to feed the baby. SISTER *holds* WHITE *by the arm; she is surprised and displeased*

SISTER Sister-in-law!

You have been here one month and   7, ang
now sorrow comes to us unplanned.   8, ang

Is there something I should understand?	9, ang
I'll fight for you if you command.	8, ang

WHITE *to* SYU'S SISTER
Dear Sister-in-law,

Little One is young and I must leave the land,	11, ang
so I ask you please to try to understand.	11, ang
Please raise him carefully with your own hand	10, ang
to be as good and honest as we had planned.	11, ang

Dear Sister-in-law, my husband will explain to you later what
has happened to me. I am disturbed that Fa Hai is destroying our
happy marriage, and I am concerned about my delicate sweet
baby! He is only one month old, and now he has to leave his
mother. Since he is your brother's flesh and blood, I beg you to
see him as your very own and raise him that way. When I die,
I shall remember your great favor and real virtue.

Sister, take my baby. It's more than I can stand.	12, ang

She hands her baby to SYU'S SISTER, *but then she takes him back
again when he begins to cry*

My poor baby.

From now on, your real mother will be your dear aunt.	12, ang

Suppressing her emotion, WHITE *hands the baby back to* SYU'S
SISTER

SYU How terrible!

Lovers struck down in this land –	7, ang
my rage does not understand.	7, ang
I regret Golden Mountain and	8, ang
following Fa Hai's command.	7, ang

FA HAI Syu Syan!

If I gave you no command,   7, ang
you would be dead by your wife's hand.   8, ang

SYU   Bah!

At long last I understand: 7, ang
I would be dead by your malicious hand!   10, ang
Break the Golden Bowl, I demand!   8, ang

He tries to break it, but fails

FA HAI   Syu Syan!

Don't fight the Buddha's high command   8, ang

Laughs

WHITE *points at* FA HAI, *shouting*

WHITE   Fa Hai, you thief! Don't you dare laugh! Do you think that the love between my husband and me can be contained in this Golden Bowl?

Fa Hai, we don't need your mirth.   7, e
All your prayers just teach you ways to slay,   9, wo
I am in this bowl today   7, wo
but I love Syu in the same way.   8, wo

FA HAI   Wei, Two, listen to my order: place this white snake under Lei Feng Tower. Unless the water runs dry from West Lake or unless Lei Feng Tower falls, she will never be able to come out again!

WHITE   What a thief!

WEI TWO *takes* WHITE *and is about to leave, when* SYU SYAN *and his sister try to save her. They are stopped by* FA HAI

SYU   *painfully*
My Lady!

SISTER Sister-in-law!

WHITE Dear husband – Sister-in-law – my baby!

The stage is dark

SCENE 16 *The Falling of the Tower*

At the mouth of the Chyan Tang River. The clouds are thick and the water is rolling heavily

BLUE, *leading the* CAVE SPIRITS, *hurriedly appears*

BLUE My troops move across the land!   7, an
I've come to South River sand,   7, an
to save White as I planned,   6, an
to beat Fa Hai hand to hand.   7, an
Golden Spears at my command!   7, an

Clouds open and both West Lake and Thunder Peak Pagoda appear

BLUE I see Thunder Peak Pagoda stand!   7, an

Hey, Tower God, come out and give yourself up!

TOWER GOD *appears with his army*

TOWER GOD You evil female demon, where have you come from? How dare you call on me?

BLUE I am the great Blue Snake! Hurry and let my Lady out, and I will spare your life.

TOWER GOD Without the order of Master Fa Hai, who would dare to let her go?

BLUE   It has been centuries since my Sister was put under Lei Feng Tower. I have been holding my tears and keeping back my sadness, so I would know how to succeed in sword fighting. I have brought all the Cave Spirits with me here today to revenge my Sister!

TOWER GOD   So it is you, Demon Blue, who have come here. Well, do not try to escape. On guard!

They both start to fight with their armies. The TOWER GOD *and his army fail and retreat.* BLUE's *army starts to burn the Tower*

BLUE   Thunder Peak Pagoda is falling, my Lady. Hurry and come out!

The tower falls and SU JEN WHITE *appears gracefully from some colorful clouds*

Curtain

LI SYAU CHWUN

The Wild Boar Forest

TRANSLATED BY
JOHN D. MITCHELL AND
DONALD CHANG

CHARACTERS

GAU CHYOU   high statesman in court

GAU SHR DE   son of GAU CHYOU

FU AN   imperial servant in GAU family

LU CHYAN   imperial servant in GAU family

LIN SHOU   old servant in the LIN family

JANG SHR   LADY JANG, LIN CHUNG's wife

LIN CHUNG   drillmaster of Imperial Court

JIN ER   LADY JANG's maid

LU JR SHEN   chivalrous monk

GAU FU   servant in GAU CHYOU's residence

GAU WANG   servant in GAU CHYOU's residence

JANG YUNG   LIN CHUNG's father-in-law

SYWE BA   guard who takes LIN CHUNG into exile

DUNG CHAU   guard who takes LIN CHUNG into exile

JANG SAN
LEE SZ
REN WU
SYN LYOU   ruffians who later become LU JR SHEN's entourage

GUARD, BANNERMAN, VEHICLE ATTENDANT, BODYGUARD, PRISON GUARD, GUARD AT THE GATE, HOUSEHOLD GUARDS, OLD SOLDIER, AN EXTRA

SCENE 1 *Home of Minister of War,* GAU CHYOU
Enter four GUARDS, *two* BANNERMEN, *and* GAU CHYOU

GAU CHYOU I am a statesman, controlling the Imperial Court.
Who does not honor and respect me?

One wrinkle of an eyebrow; a thousand plots are hatched;
The tongue kills; I don't use a sword.
Years past in the Ywan Clan I was a fellow of no importance;
In one step I reached heights, overshadowing all in Court.

This old fellow is Gau Chyou!
In the great Sung Dynasty I serve the Emperor Dau Jyun as
    Minister of War.
How irritating is drillmaster Lin Chung, in charge of 800,000
    Imperial Guards – a man high and mighty in military
    skills.
I had the intention of taking him under my wing.
Who would have thought that he would shun me – except at
    Court affairs!
This vexes me.

GAU SHR DE *offstage*
Ah, hah! *Enter* GAU SHR DE *with* GAU FU. *Onstage sings*
I've just been in the study,
Feeling bored;
I think I'll go out into the streets
To ease my heart a bit.

To his father

Say, 'Pop,' you've just come back! *

GAU CHYOU You're not at work in the study. What brings you here?

GAU SHR DE The teacher didn't come today. I'm planning to go out and amuse
myself a while. How about some money?

* The Chinese word *Dye* is Peking slang, familiar, and like the English
'Pop.'

GAU CHYOU *signaling to an attendant*
Come.

BANNERMAN Present.

GAU CHYOU Fetch fifty ounces of pure silver.

BANNERMAN *getting a package of silver and handing it to* GAU FU
It is done!

GAU CHYOU *to his son*
Don't get into trouble outside; go early, and return early.

GAU SHR DE Enough of that! Don't worry.

> GAU CHYOU *exits with a vigorous turn and gesture, followed by* BANNERMEN

GAU SHR DE *to the servant*
Ask Fu An and Lu Chyan to come here.

GAU FU Fu An, Lu Chyan, come.

FU AN AND
LU CHYAN *entering*
Young Master. *They bow before* GAU SHR DE

GAU SHR DE Enough!

FU AN AND
LU CHYAN We've been called: What are your wishes?

GAU SHR DE I'm bored to death! Where does one go to have some fun?

LU CHYAN What a perfect coincidence: today is no other day but the twenty-eighth day of the Fourth Month; the very day that the Dung Ywe Temple opens. We'll go there and look around. How does that strike you?

GAU SHR DE Dung Ywe Temple . . . *To a stage attendant*
Boy, tell them to bring my horse and wait.

FU AN AND
   GAU FU Stable boys, bring the horse to await the master.

GAU SHR DE *sings*
    My father's awe
    Intimidates the Minister of State.
    His awesome air, so shivering,
    Overpowers the highest in the Court.

    Someone bring my horse! I'm off to the Festival Grounds. *He
    mimes mounting his horse, and continues to sing*

    Those who obey, thrive!
    Those who disobey, die!
    Out of my way, Wa!

    All exit

SCENE 2 *In front of Dung Ywe Temple. In performance, in front of an
     act curtain, downstage*

LIN CHUNG *offstage, sings*
    The morning sun is high,*
    Clear breezes turn.

    Enter LIN SHOU, *old servant in the Lin family,* JIN ER, *maid; a*
    VEHICLE ATTENDANT; LADY JANG; LIN CHUNG

    Trees dot the green wilderness;
    A hundred birds sing.

* The Chinese text is literally 'the rising sun has reached the third pole.'
As a Chinese device for marking time, it means that measured by the third
pole it would be 10:00 A.M.

LADY JANG* *continues to sing*
Because I was ill, I took a vow –

She is interrupted by her husband

LIN CHUNG To go to Dung Ywe Temple to give thanks
That Divine Spirits have blessed us with your recovery.
On the journey we were not able
To enjoy fully all the beautiful places.
Suddenly we've reached Dung Ywe Temple.

Ah, my lady, we have already come here before Dung Ywe Temple. I have a desire to enjoy the Festival awhile. My lady, what do you think?

LADY JANG *points to her servant,* JIN ER
In that case, let us go to the temple to burn incense. We'll wait for you. That's my thought.

LIN CHUNG Fine, fine, fine.
Lin Shou, take over the horse and wait upon my lady.

LIN SHOU Yes.

LIN CHUNG *sings*
I, a man's man,
Ranked below *that* Gau Chyou
Have limitless bitterness;
I'll ease my mind
As I face leisure flowers and wild grass.†

They exit separately

* Lin Chung's wife is referred to in the text by her maiden name as Lady Jang.
† A more literal translation of the Chinese text would be: 'I'll expand my chest as I face leisure flowers and wild grass.' The phrase leisure flowers and wild grass alludes poetically to the entertainment at the temple festival sites.

SCENE 3 *The vegetable garden of Syang Gwo Monastery. The scenery consists of a section of wall, with a piece broken out of it, and a willow tree.*

LU JR SHEN *offstage*
Amitabha!

Sings and enters

I am dependent on other people;
It is difficult to do as I please.
I'm only able to walk in the vegetable garden.

Hey, just because back there on Wu Tai Mountain I took to drink, and under the influence of wine broke the mountain gate; my teacher said the place was not big enough for the two of us; so right then and there he wrote a letter, telling me to come here to Syang Gwo Monastery. The old Buddhist priest here, on the other hand, doesn't care if I drink or eat meat; his only demand is that every day I water and keep an eye on the vegetable garden . . . Hey! hey! I'm bored to death.

Sings

That year out West, I wounded someone;
To avoid trouble I ran away and took on the monk's habit.
Simply because of lust for the cup,
I brought down on my head this mishap;
My master sent 'yours truly' to this place.
Just a moment ago the old one talked to me,
Telling me that there were always thieves in the vegetable
        garden;
As for this good guy here!
Who are they to oppose *me!*
Hey!

He mimes watering the garden

Every day, bearing water,
Sprinkling vegetables
Drives me out of my mind.

Ah . . . hey, hey! Truly, now having eaten, I hanker for a nap. I've an idea: by that tree I'll nap for a spell. What's wrong with that?

Four clown characters enter *

JANG SAN Hey there! Brothers, do you remember all that I told you?

LI SZ AND
   OTHERS *in unison*
Remembered! *Tapping their foreheads*

JANG SAN When we go over there, watch for my wink. As soon as I grab his arms, tackle him, hold him down on the ground, and sock him: then let him go.

LI SZ AND
   OTHERS *in unison*
Right!

JANG SAN Brothers, what a break! There's the monk, sleeping.

LI SZ Let me grab his arms.

REN WU AND
   SYU LYOU *in unison*
I'll grab his legs.

JANG SAN What's this about 'grabbing arms, legs.' He's asleep! *Smirking* Brothers won't it look like we're beating up a helpless person! Take your cue from me. As soon as I hold his arms, you'll grab his legs and hit him.

LU JR SHEN *waking up and rising*
Hey, what're you sneaking around here for? Thinking you might steal some vegetables? Right?

JANG SAN Oh! Oh! Master, we brothers are not *here* to steal vegetables.

* These four characters are named in Chinese in a manner that suggests the English equivalent of 'Tom, Dick, and Harry.'

LU JR SHEN   What *are* you doing?

JANG SAN   We heard you're in charge of the vegetable garden here, *so* we brothers came to congratulate you.

LI SZ AND OTHERS   Right! We came to congratulate you.

LU JR SHEN   Oh, is that so. Well may I ask what are your names?

JANG SAN   I'm called Jang San.

LI SZ   I'm called Li Sz.

REN WU   I'm called Ren Wu.

SYU LYOU   I'm Syu Lyou.

LU JR SHEN   Oh, now I know who you four fellows are. Amitabha.

JANG SAN AND OTHERS   Ah! *The four attack* LU JR SHEN, *off guard*

LU JR SHEN   Ah! What's the idea?

JANG SAN   Just this: ever since you came, we brothers haven't been able to get any vegetables. Today we've got to beat you up.

OTHERS   *in unison*
Today we've got to beat you up.

LU JR SHEN   Ah! From your boasts, I gather you're going to try your strength with me.

JANG SAN AND OTHERS   Ah! We've got to beat you up.

LU JR SHEN   Good. Who has the guts to come out and play with me! Hunh! See what I'll do to you blind sons-of-bitches! Day in and day out you take advantage of meek monks, but today you've run into 'yours truly' and you'll get what's coming to you! *As the four try to hold him down,* LU JR SHEN, *with a shake, throws them to the ground*

JANG SAN   Ay, ya! Ay, ya! Master, can we brothers call it quits!

LU JR SHEN   So you give in?

JANG SAN   Yes, yes.

LU JR SHEN   Are you scared of me now?

JANG SAN   Afraid of you – yes!

LU JR SHEN   I'm letting you off cheaply.

JANG SAN   *to his followers*
How come none of you made a move?

LI SZ AND
REN WU   *together*
Who didn't make a move?

LU JR SHEN   Today I really did let you off easily.

To REN WU

As a punishment *you* go to Front Street: buy wine.

To SYU LYOU

And *you* go to Back Street and buy meat. When you return: 'Yours truly' will get roaring drunk! Hurry it up!

JANG SAN   Yes, yes. *To his followers*
Hurry it up and buy the wine and meat.

Exit SYU LYOU *and* REN WU; *softly to* LI SZ

You see, this monk truly has power.

LI SZ   We brothers who bum around all day should learn from this. This could happen again. We'll have to do something about it.

JANG SAN   You're right. I have a good mind to follow him.

Points to the monk

I might learn some tricks from him. How do you like the idea?

LI SZ   I don't know whether he's willing or not.

JANG SAN   That's all right. We'll discuss it with him a bit.

LI SZ   Discuss it with him.

JANG SAN   Say, we brothers want to reform and follow you as our teacher. We want to learn your military skills. Don't say anything. Just agree to teach us.

LU JR SHEN   Fine! Give up your evil ways; follow the good. I'll teach you.

Enter REN WU *and* SYU LYOU

Ah yes the delicious liquor is on the way: Meat and drink are here! Ha! Ha!

JANG SAN   Good, good, good. Right here and now we will honor you as our teacher.

JANG SAN
AND OTHERS   Teacher, we little brothers are bowing to you.

The four kneel and bow with their foreheads to the ground to LU JR SHEN.

LU JR SHEN   Ai ya, ya! *Surprised*
No need to bow, no need to bow. Get up, get up. Ha! Ha! Ha! Men, lay out this delicious meat and drink under the big tree. Let's sit on the ground and *drink!* Ah!

While all are drinking amiably, there is a sound of a bird flying over head.

LU JR SHEN *sings*
> We're busy gulping a thousand cups of delicious wine;
> I heard a bird up in a tree, cawing.

A sound effect from the orchestra, imitating the sound of crows – LU JR SHEN notices bird droppings in his cup

> Hey! Dirty things are falling into our cups. Truly it's discouraging.

JANG SAN   Master, up in this tree is an old crow's nest. He keeps shitting on us; it's really irritating – say, brothers; let's get a ladder. *About to leave*

LU JR SHEN   What are you going to use it for?

JANG SAN   We'll move the ladder, climb the tree, cut off all the branches; the crow won't be able to build a nest, so he'll not be able to shit on us.

LU JR SHEN   Cut off the branches? What's the point of that?

JANG SAN
AND OTHERS   Master, so, what would you do?

LU JR SHEN   Why not pull up the tree! Isn't it a case of: to get rid of weeds you uproot 'em.

JANG SAN
AND OTHERS   Oh! Pull it . . . pull out the tree! When trees are big, the roots go deep. Talk about pulling it out, even to saw it takes a long time. Master, you couldn't even budge it.

LU JR SHEN   Your teacher said it; he can do it!

JANG SAN
AND OTHERS   You're able to pull out the tree, hunh! We don't believe it!

LU JR SHEN   I figured that you wouldn't believe me. Make way now! *He first shakes the tree, vigorously pulls at it, finally he succeeds in uprooting the tree*

Ha, ha, ha!

The four of them are stunned, motionless as if statues; LU JR SHEN *calls to them*

Hunh! Men, men, hey, men! *He throws the tree aside*

JANG SAN   Brothers, now you see how great our master's strength is! Such a thick tree: he pulled it out in no time at all.

He points to LI SZ

Ai ya, if your neck fell into his hands, he'd stretch it as if it were a noodle. What skill!

LU JR SHEN   That's not so great! Why if I just wield my Zen staff, neither wind nor rain can touch me.

JANG SAN
AND OTHERS   Hey, master, why don't you show us some tricks? Let us brothers see what we've never seen before!

LU JR SHEN   Fine. Go to the back yard for my staff: lift it up, and bring it to me.

Sings

When my fist strikes South Mountain
Fierce tigers die;
I dare to kick the dragon –
– Now I hurriedly twirl my staff a few times.

He twirls staff

LIN CHUNG   *enters, stands on the other side of the wall, fascinated. He watches the scene through a break in the wall upstage*

What skill with the staff! *He continues the singing, finishing* LU JR SHEN's *line*

Taught by a famous teacher,
He has a singular talent.

LU JR SHEN *and his four cronies look at* LIN CHUNG

LU JR SHEN   Please, come over, come over!

LIN CHUNG   Ai ya, ya. I observe that brother's military skills are uncommon. Your art with a staff is fantastic! I'm full of admiration.

LU JR SHEN   Mm, from what you say, could it be that you also shine in this line.

LIN CHUNG   Ai ya, ya. I've just got my foot in the door. I don't match you, brother, by a lot.

LU JR SHEN   You flatter me, you flatter me! Please may I know your name?

LIN CHUNG   I am 'Leopard-Head' Lin Chung.

LU JR SHEN   *happily surprised*
Oh, you are that very drillmaster for military arts, Lin Chung, who's in charge of 800,000 Imperial Guards.

LIN CHUNG   Right! That's exactly who I am!

LU JR SHEN   Ai ya, ya. For a long time I've been wanting to meet you, ah, hah, wanting to meet you.

LIN CHUNG   You have flattered me. Please, brother, what's your name. Where are you from? *

LU JR SHEN   I'm Lu Jr Shen, from Yen An district.

* In the Chinese Lin Chung's request for Lu Jr Shen's name is phrased acknowledging that Lu Jr Shen as a monk would have picked a religious name in place of his given name.

LIN CHUNG   *happily surprised*
You are that very Deputy Lu of the West?

LU JR SHEN   *excitedly*
You flatter *me*. I am that very one.

LIN CHUNG   Ai ya, ya. I've longed to meet you, brother: your name thunders out West; your swordsmanship and honor are matchless! I am lucky to have come to know you, the hero; I must have been good in three of my past lives to be so fortunate. Ha ha!

LU JR SHEN   You flatter me! Ha! Ha! . . .

     LU JR SHEN *and* LIN CHUNG *laugh heartily;* LU JR SHEN *nods his head, indicating he's extremely excited and extremely happy*

LIN CHUNG   Brother, there's something I want to say, and I don't know whether I should or not?

LU JR SHEN   What words of gold do you have; quickly, quickly. Say them!

LIN CHUNG   I have the intention of raising myself to be your blood brother.

LU JR SHEN   *surprised that he has the same thought*
Oh! I've had the exact, same idea, but you said it first.

LIN CHUNG   Ai ya, ya, since I have the honor of your not rejecting me, let's state the date of our births.

LU JR SHEN   This year I am thirty-two years old.

LIN CHUNG   I've passed twenty-eight empty springs.

LU JR SHEN   So now you are my virtuous younger brother.

LIN CHUNG   You are *my* benevolent older brother!

LU JR SHEN   Younger brother!

LIN CHUNG   Older brother!

LU JR SHEN Uh!

LIN CHUNG Ah! *Both laugh heartily*
Ha, ha, . . . let us bow to the heavens.

They kneel, clasp their fists, raise them to their foreheads, and bow to the heavens

LU JR SHEN *sings*
We swear to be close as hand and foot.*

LIN CHUNG *continues singing*
We'll share, equally, happiness and hardship.

LU JR SHEN As close as if suckled by the same mother.

LIN CHUNG The fame of our timeless friendship
Will be glorified again and again.

They rise and resume dialogue

Benevolent older brother let younger brother bow to you. *He bows deeply*

LU JR SHEN You flatter me, you flatter me. *To* JANG SAN *and others*

Come over here, come over here, meet and bow before your 'uncle.' †

JANG SAN
AND OTHERS We bow before you, uncle. *They bow*

LIN CHUNG *hurriedly tries to stop them*
You flatter me, you flatter me.

LU JR SHEN It's right for you to receive their homage. These are my followers. Oh, ha, ha, . . . for a long time I have heard, Virtuous

* The two Chinese characters for hand and foot are used for a compound phrase meaning: a blood relationship; e.g., members of the same family.
† The Chinese word *shr shu* seems best rendered as uncle in English.

Brother, that your military arts are extraordinary; do I dare to trouble you to show us a bit of your skill; so we can look up to you.

LIN CHUNG Ai ya, ya, in front of Benevolent Brother? How will I, a younger brother dare to make a fool of myself!

LU JR SHEN You're overly modest, you're overly modest.

JANG SAN Young master, we have all kinds of weapons here. Why don't you practice a bit; let us men watch. How about it?

LIN CHUNG Well, I'm going to make a fool of myself!

LU JR SHEN What weapon do you use?

LIN CHUNG Well, in that case then, fetch a sword.

LU JR SHEN *to* JANG SAN *and others*
Fine, quickly, bring a sword here.

JANG SAN Yes, master. *Hands the sword to* LIN CHUNG

LIN CHUNG Here goes!

Sings

Here's the amateur
Showing off before experts.
Just take a look!
I have the audacity to talk of clubs and spears.
I loosen my robe,
Point my sword;
It fills the air with a cold, white light.

LIN CHUNG *shows off his swordmanship;* LU JR SHEN *looks on, fascinated*

Fine! Fine!

LU JR SHEN Fine!

Sings

As expected,
Your military arts are extraordinary.

LIN CHUNG You flatter me.

LU JR SHEN Good, good, you are good, ha, ha.

> LIN CHUNG's *wife's maid,* JIN ER, *enters, running. Upon seeing* LIN CHUNG *she goes right to him*

JIN ER At last I've found you! Something terrible has happened.

LIN CHUNG *alarmed*
Why this panic?

JIN ER While mistress was offering incense at Dung Ywe Temple, a gang of ruffians came and accosted us; you'd better hurry and see what's happened.

LIN CHUNG *greatly alarmed*
How is it possible? Quickly take me there – Brother Lu, something has happened to my wife. Some other day I'll receive your instruction; now I take my leave. LIN CHUNG *and* JIN ER *exit hurriedly*

LU JR SHEN Hold it! If Virtuous Brother goes off alone, he'll be attacked, I fear. Men!

JANG SAN Here!

LU JR SHEN Follow your teacher! Let's beat up those sons of bitches!

JANG SAN
AND OTHERS Let's go!

> LU JR SHEN *exits with his four followers*

SCENE 4 *Dung Ywe Temple. Performed in front of an act curtain*

LADY JANG *sings offstage*
In the temple I ran into ruffians;
My mind is unsettled, my heart aflutter.

Distraught, she runs on stage; LIN SHOU *follows, trying to protect her;* GAU SHR DE, FU AN, LU CHYAN *and the four bodyguards enter, chasing* LADY JANG. *With a fan,* LU CHYAN *masks his face.* LADY JANG *runs in circles*

In broad daylight
They made advances toward me, a mere woman;
For what reason?
For life or death, I must go quickly!

LIN SHOU *to* GAU SHR DE, *singing*
For what reason are you abusing this lady?

Dialogue

Madmen, you keep on molesting a lady. Do you mean to tell me that you do not fear the Emperor's law!

GAU SHR DE Shut up! You're meddling in my affairs. I'm going to kill you. Come. *He signals to his bodyguards*
Grab him, ah, ha, ha! *Turning to* LADY JANG Young lady, a moment ago I told you; if you yield to me, you will have endless luxury, wealth without limit. Little lady I guess you'll not reject the proposal . . . ha, ha, . . .

LADY JANG *slaps* GAU SHR DE
What a sneak!

Sings

Madman, how dare you!
What gall you have!
With sweet talk
You molest me.

I was born a pure and chaste girl.
How do you expect me to come down to *your* level.
You keep on being fresh!
Do you not at all fear
Payment and punishment in the next life! *
I advise you to give up at once what you have in mind.
Otherwise, I'll take you before a court official.

GAU SHR DE Ha, ha! I tried to persuade you with kind words; you're stubborn and don't listen. I'm going to be rough now. Wa!

Sings to his servants

Come forward,
Hurry up,
Grab the bride for me.
Grab her!

Just as GAU SHR DE *is about to grab her,* LIN CHUNG *and* JIN ER
enter, LIN CHUNG *pushes away* GAU SHR DE. *Losing his balance,*
GAU SHR DE *almost falls but is caught by* FU AN

LIN CHUNG *continues the singing*
What's the meaning
Of your bold and bad behavior?

You try to take this lady; what punishment fits your crime?

LU CHYAN *recognizing* LIN CHUNG, *he comes between* LIN CHUNG *and* GAU
SHR DE
Oh! I see it's brother Lin.

LIN CHUNG *recognizing the Minister of War's son,* GAU SHR DE, *he is taken
aback*
Oh . . .

LU CHYAN Virtuous Brother, don't act so impulsively. *Pointing to* GAU
SHR DE
Young master is here.

* The Buddhistic idea of Karma or rebirth.

LIN CHUNG   Ahh – ahh. *Stops in his tracks*

GAU SHR DE   Ah, ha! What gall you have, Lin Chung! How dare you defy me! You deserve to die! You deserve to die! It's a crime that deserves ten thousand deaths!

LIN CHUNG   *although angry inside, he has no choice but to suppress his feelings under the circumstances*
I, Lin Chung, actually didn't know that you, Young Master, were here. I've much offended you. This woman is my wife. She was pestered in the street. Would you tell me that I should stand idly by?

GAU SHR DE   It matters not to me what she is to you! I see she's good: I want to take her for my wife. The fact that you're in my way: I say this is no good.

LIN CHUNG   Hey! While Lin Chung is here, you are not going to get away with this.

GAU SHR DE   Who do you think you are, Lin Chung? If it were not that my father had pushed you up the ladder would you be where you are today? What is this? Now that you've wings, you think you can fly! * How dare you not listen to what I am saying. If I don't get tough with you, you won't respect my rank.

To his followers

Come, take him away.

LU CHYAN   *quickly trying to stop* GAU SHR DE
Young Master, don't, don't.

GAU SHR DE   I will it! Take him away, take him away! I will it, I will it . . .

* In the Chinese, the expression is literally: 'Are your wings getting hard?' It suggests that the person is growing up and now wishes to fly and be independent.

LU CHYAN *to* LIN CHUNG

Virtuous Brother, I think that what happened today really comes from a misunderstanding. I see that it is already late. For the time being, Virtuous Brother, please return to your home; tomorrow young master and I will come there to apologize and to ask forgiveness – that's all.

GAU SHR DE No such thing: take him away, take him away!

LU CHYAN Virtuous Brother, how about it?

LIN CHUNG As a favor to you, Captain Lu, I'll let it pass.

GAU SHR DE How is it you're not taking him away? No matter who it is, he can't stop me in this.

LU CHYAN *whispers and gestures to* GAU SHR DE

All right, all right, that's that!

GAU SHR DE *pauses and turns from* LU CHYAN *to* LIN CHUNG

Lin Chung, let me tell you this: I pardon you because this is your first offense: Next time you cross me I'll take your life.

To GUARDS

Come! Let's go!

LU JR SHEN, *the monk, enters with his four followers*

LU JR SHEN Men, charge!

The four BODYGUARDS, LU CHYAN, *and* FU AN *exit, running*

Daring dog's head, how dare you abuse my brother. LU JR SHEN *grabs* GAU SHR DE, *forcing him to the ground.*

Is it possible that you're not afraid of dying? *He shakes* GAU SHR DE *vigorously*

LIN CHUNG   *comes forward hurriedly*
Benevolent Brother, this is the son of the Minister of War, General Gau. I hope that Benevolent Brother will be generous and forgive him.

LU JR SHEN   I don't care, General or no General, let me kill this worm. *He raises his fist;* LIN CHUNG *stops him hurriedly*

LIN CHUNG   As a favor to Little Brother, forgive.

LU JR SHEN   Virtuous Brother, for your sake, just now I forgive this dog's head! *To* GAU SHR DE

Let me put a question to you. In the future: will you dare to behave like this? *He shakes him vigorously*

GAU SHR DE   *whining*
Ai ya, I won't do it again.

LU JR SHEN   If you don't change your bad ways, and you bump into 'your – priest – grandfather,' – Lu Jr Shen, you'd better stop thinking about living. LU JR SHEN *shakes him even harder*

GAU SHR DE   *in unbearable pain*
Ai ya, come now, come now, quickly, let me go: my priest – ancestor!

LU JR SHEN   Beat it! * Get lost, you mother's – *He lets go of* GAU SHR DE

GAU SHR DE   Ai, ya. *He rises. Suddenly he regains his usual attitude of contempt.* Tu! † You daring, crazy monk. I didn't expect you to be so ill mannered. Guard!

Guards have left. The ones standing behind him are LU JR SHEN'S *followers*

Ai, ya!

* The Chinese expression is literally 'roll like an egg.'
† A Chinese sound to express contempt.

JANG SAN
AND OTHERS Beat him up!

GAU SHR DE Don't! *Exits hurriedly*

LU JR SHEN *turns to* LIN CHUNG
Virtuous Brother, wouldn't it have been simpler, if a moment
ago with one blow I had sent him to his death? Why did you
stop me?

LIN CHUNG *sighs*
Hai! I am subject to the Minister of War, General Gau; as for
today's affair, I hold my fists, keep back my words. Shame is killing me.

LU JR SHEN Virtuous Brother, my advice to you is to quit your job and get
out. Avoid other people's breath!

LIN CHUNG Well . . . the only thing is those eight hundred thousand fellow
soldiers; how can I stand to part from them?

LU JR SHEN You worry too much!

LIN CHUNG *turns to* LADY JANG
Ah, my Lady. This is Benevolent Brother Lu. A moment ago I
became his blood brother. Come and meet him.

LADY JANG Benevolent Brother Lu, may I wish you ten thousand happi-
nesses. *Bows*

LU JR SHEN Virtuous Brother, is this then the wife of my blood brother?

LIN CHUNG Just so, this is my wife!

LU JR SHEN Ah – well – I am to return the courtesy – ah. *With hands to his
forehead, making a Buddhist salute*

Amitabha!

LIN CHUNG Please, Benevolent Brother, come visit my humble home and
chat a bit. How about it?

LU JR SHEN   I was just about to visit you. *To his followers* You – you all go home – master's going off but will be right back.

JANG SAN
AND OTHERS   It'll be done. *They exit*

LIN CHUNG   Benevolent Brother, please! LIN CHUNG *motions to him to proceed ahead*

LU JR SHEN   *sings*
              Within my breast stir a thousand hatreds.

LIN CHUNG   *continues the singing*
              Under Gau Chyou's thumb it's hard to breathe! *

              All exit

SCENE 5 GAU CHYOU'S *Palace.* GAU CHYOU *enters with two* BANNERMEN

GAU CHYOU   *sings*
              My position is high,
              My title is well known;
              People look up to me;
              My awe-inspiring air
              Causes such shudders
              That the court officials tremble.
              It is irritating that Lin Chung makes it difficult
              For me to realize my ambition.

              He sits. GAU SHR DE *enters with his arm in a sling;* GAU FU *follows*

GAU SHR DE   Ai ya, it's killing me!

---

* In the Chinese the expression is literally 'under the fence of.'

GAU CHYOU Ah? Why is my son in such a state?

GAU SHR DE I almost got beaten to death!

GAU CHYOU Hunh! I figured you had behaved badly; so you've really been beat up; am I right or not?

GAU SHR DE *I* behaved badly? On the contrary, is seeking a marriage behaving badly? You see, I had a rough time, and you do nothing about it. Instead, you scold me; I'm not going to talk to you. I'm going to look for Mama. *Starts to leave*

GAU CHYOU Come back! Since it was a matter of marriage, tell Father; that will make it easier for me to help you out.

GAU SHR DE That's better. Just listen to what I tell you; I took my man and went to Dung Ywe Temple to stroll about. I saw a girl. No need to say how beautiful she was. I mentioned marriage, but she didn't yield; she came over and slapped me! They called over some 'bums.' * Almost beat me to death! Think of something.

GAU CHYOU Wait. Father'll send someone over there to talk about the marriage. I figure they would not dare *not* to agree – but I do not know to what family she belongs?

GAU SHR DE Actually she's not a stranger.

GAU CHYOU Well, who is she?

GAU SHR DE It's the wife of Lin Chung.

GAU CHYOU Since it's Lin Chung's wife, how can you marry her?

GAU SHR DE So what! I don't care; I've got to marry her! Are you going to get her for me or aren't you? If I don't marry her, I'll kill myself and I mean it! † Let me tell you: I'm your only child! You think about this: Who means more to you? Lin Chung or me?

* It is slang in Chinese: *tu hwen hwen.*
† In Chinese: 'If I say I die, then I die.'

GAU CHYOU Ai ya, stop! Let me think!

To himself

If I seize this opportunity, Lin Chung will be wiped out; my son's marriage at the same time will be made. Isn't it killing two birds with one stone? *

To GAU SHR DE

Son, as your father I consent. But I have no idea how to carry it out.

GAU SHR DE It doesn't matter. Fu An and Lu Chyan long ago thought of a plan.

GAU CHYOU *greatly pleased*
Hmm!

To a servant

Tell them to come forward.

GAU SHR DE *withdraws to the side of the stage*

GAU FU Fu An, Lu Chyan come forth!

FU AN AND
LU CHYAN *enter and kneel*
Our respects to the Minister. What are the orders?

GAU CHYOU Rise. My son wants to marry Lin Chung's wife. You two fellows, what scheme do you have?

LU CHYAN I've a plan here all right.

GAU CHYOU What marvelous plan do you have?

* Literally in Chinese it is 'One raising of the hand, two gains.'

LU CHYAN *whispers*
Minister . . .

GAU CHYOU *after hearing it, looks around, pretending to be surprised*
Who'd have the heart to carry out such a vicious scheme!

LU CHYAN Minister, do you mean to tell me that you've forgotten?

GAU CHYOU Ah?

LU CHYAN As long as Lin Chung, drillmaster of the Imperial Guards, remains; how can you, your lordship, realize your heart's desire
and do what *you* want to do!

GAU CHYOU Hmm! . . . Go ahead. Do it according to this plan. *With a
vigorous turn and gesture, he exits*

LU CHYAN All will be done as you say.

GAU SHR DE How goes it?

LU CHYAN It's done.

GAU SHR DE Fine . . . Fellows,* bring here the minister's precious sword.

To Gau Fu

Call Gau Wang.

FU AN Gau Wang, come forth.

GAU WANG *offstage*
Coming. *Enters* My respects to young master. What are your
orders?

GAU SHR DE Gau Wang, you are ordered to pose as a man selling swords. –
Take the Minister's precious sword with you. If you meet Lin
Chung, you then . . . lend me your ear. *Whispers*

* In the Chinese the words are *syau dz;* the closest equivalent is our slang
word in English, 'punks.'

GAU WANG   Your orders will be carried out. *Exits with the sword*

LU CHYAN   Ha, ha, ha. What do you think of this scheme?

GAU SHR DE   A fine plot. Go have a drink with me.

LU CHYAN   At this moment? How do I have time to go have a drink?

GAU SHR DE   Just what are you going to do now?

LU CHYAN   I still have something to do for you.

GAU SHR DE   Right, right, right! Get going. I'll be waiting for you. Then come back quickly, come back quickly. *Both exit, separately*

SCENE 6   *In the street. Performed before an act curtain, front stage*

LU JR SHEN *and* LIN CHUNG *enter*

LU JR SHEN   *sings*
With wine and song
We're having a riotous time.

LIN CHUNG   *continues singing*
I drink to forget,
But anger is difficult to suppress.

LU JR SHEN   *continues singing*
Arm in arm
We enter the big street.

GAU WANG   *offstage*
Swords to sell!

LIN CHUNG   *continues to sing*
I hear someone shouting that he's selling swords!

GAU WANG *enters with sword*
What a pity! In this big town of Byan Lyang, there isn't even one who knows precious swords. Truly, truly pitiable!

LIN CHUNG This fellow, keeps shouting that he's selling swords. May I have a look?

GAU WANG Please.

LIN CHUNG *taking the sword*
Let me take a look.

Pauses

To be sure it *is* a precious sword. I don't know how much you're asking for it?

GAU WANG One thousand strings of cash.

LIN CHUNG Well, are you able to part with it for only twenty ounces of pure silver?

GAU WANG Since you, a swordsman, know precious swords, it doesn't matter how little the price. I'll give it to a hero!

LIN CHUNG Good, good, good!

Giving the silver, he takes the sword

Now that I have it, may I ask where *you* got it?

GAU WANG It's none other than an inheritance from my forebears.

LIN CHUNG May I ask your name?

GAU WANG *hesitates*
Well . . .

Recites

When people meet by chance,
There's no need to give names.

Exits

LIN CHUNG *continues the reciting*
Should a hero be enslaved by worldly things,
He deserves pity! *

Benevolent Brother, this *is* a precious sword; come, take a look!
Come, take a look, Benevolent Brother.

LU JR SHEN *looking at the sword*
Let your older brother take a look. Wow! Truly it *is* a rare
thing! Virtuous Brother, since ancient times, it has always been:
rouge for the beauties: swords for the righteous. So now it can
be said this sword has met its true owner!

LIN CHUNG You flatter me.

LU JR SHEN Your getting this precious sword is cause to rejoice, deserves
celebrating. Let's you and I go back to the vegetable garden and
really drink to celebrate the happy occasion.

LIN CHUNG Well: fine, fine, fine! But please, Benevolent Brother, you return
home first; Little Brother will follow after immediately.

LU JR SHEN Your elder brother will be waiting at the vegetable garden for
you; then we'll drink. Virtuous Brother, come right away! Ha,
ha . . .

Sings

To celebrate
Virtuous Brother's getting a precious sword
Is really a joy . . .

Exits

* In the Chinese it is, literally, closer to 'when a hero is entrapped in
worldly things, he deserves pity.'

SCENE 7   LIN CHUNG's *home. Upstage curtains open, revealing large paint-ing center;* LIN CHING *mimes knocking on a door; his servant* LIN SHOU *mimes opening a door;* LIN CHUNG *mimes entering and hands sword to* LIN CHOU

LIN CHUNG   When I get home, I'll tell my wife of my good luck. Ha! Ha! *All sit*

LADY JANG   My lord, why are you laughing?

LIN CHUNG   Just a moment ago on the way I bought a precious sword. From now on, when I have a sword fight, it'll be smooth sailing!

       Sings

       Here on the road
       I got the precious sword
       Of my heart's desire;
       I'd make it difficult,
       For even a thousand soldiers,
       Had they wings to fly.

LU CHYAN   *enters, aside*
       I'm on my way!

       Sings

       I've set in motion the plot
       To cage the water dragon,
       Tie up the tiger!
       Even the God who knows the future
       Will find it difficult to know
       The outcome.

       What gentleman is at the gate?

LIN SHOU   Who's there? Oh, Mr Lu, what brings *you* here?

LU CHYAN   Is Drillmaster Lin at home?

LIN SHOU Well . . .

LU CHYAN Ah, I'm under the orders of the Minister of War; there is an important matter to be discussed!

LIN SHOU Oh, oh! Please wait for a minute. *He goes to report to* LIN CHUNG
I beg to report, Master, that Nobleman Lu begs a meeting.

LIN CHUNG Nobleman Lu Chyan?

LIN SHOU Indeed.

LADY JANG Husband, if Lu Chyan's here, it must be something.

LIN CHUNG My lady, withdraw –

To LIN SHOU

Go tell him that I greet him.

LADY JANG *and* JIN ER *exit*

LIN SHOU *to* LU CHYAN
Master greets you.

LIN CHUNG *looking about and into the air*
Where is brother Lu?

LU CHYAN *looking about for* LIN CHUNG *
Where is Virtuous Brother?

LIN CHUNG *They finally meet, bowing to each other*
Brother Lu is it? . . . Ah, ha, ha! †

LIN CHUNG Brother Lu, please sit down, it's an honor to have you in my house . . . you must come with some instruction and good advice. *They sit*

* Lin Chung is letting the audience and Lu Chyan know that they are not intimate friends and that he is creating a distance between them.
† This section is very ceremonial.

LU CHYAN That matter in the past . . . the Dung Ywe Temple . . . affair, the Minister of War knows about it. Right then and there, he gave young Master a big scolding, and for his wrong doing he ordered your 'foolish brother' to come over to your house to apologize.

LIN CHUNG *coldly*
It's all in the past; why trouble the Minister of War about it?

LU CHYAN First of all, I come to apologize for the wrong and secondly, to congratulate you.

LIN CHUNG What happiness are you talking about?

LU CHYAN Virtuous Brother, you are the hero of this generation; your military arts are superior to all. Now on top of all that you also possess a precious sword. Truly this matter of your getting this sword is like:

A dragon going back to water;
A tiger sprouting wings.
One can say that from now
You will have no equal under the heavens.

LIN CHUNG You flatter me too much – My getting the sword has just happened within a few minutes. Brother Lu, how do you know about it?

LU CHYAN Ah, within this Eastern Capital, what person does not know of you, the hero. Just a moment ago, you, Virtuous Brother, bought in the main street the sword. Someone was nearby, and saw it; immediately he reported it to the Minister of War. When the Minister of War knew about it, of course he was extremely happy for you. For that reason he ordered 'foolish brother' to come to your house, to invite you to bring the sword to his house, to compare it with his precious sword.

LIN CHUNG That thing which I bought, it does not exceed the common. How does one dare to compare it with the precious sword of the Minister of War?

LU CHYAN   Mm! . . . Why is Virtuous Brother so stubborn! I think that the Minister of War is a man who likes warriors, but if Virtuous Brother is stubborn and unwilling to go, isn't it a fact that you'd be disappointing the Minister of War?

LIN CHUNG   Brother Lu, what you say makes sense – Lin Shou, go fetch the precious sword and bring it here.

LIN SHOU   *brings the sword to him*
The precious sword is here.

LIN CHUNG   *hides his fears*
Brother Lu, the precious sword is here; so may I trouble Brother Lu just to take the sword there, for the Minister of War to look at it?

LU CHYAN   Do I hear Virtuous Brother's words? Do you mean to tell me that you're not willing to go see the Minister?

LIN CHUNG   Well . . . I have another official matter to attend to; please forgive me for not keeping you company.

LU CHYAN   Virtuous Brother, you *should* know, this is the Minister of War's order . . . Virtuous Brother. *He laughs malevolently*

One takes commands
As well as commands! *

Then and only then is he an exceptional person. Hai! Perhaps you and I are unfortunate: placed lower than we deserve, and under a Gau Chyou: so we have no choice but to suppress anger, swallow the sound. – Take my advice, Virtuous Brother, go to Gau Chyou this time; when the opportunity presents itself, we, brothers, will resign and return to our homelands; we'll serve under nobody, subservient to no one! This is 'foolish brother's' words from the bottom of his heart. I do not know what Younger Brother thinks?

* The Chinese translates literally as 'a man must be able to bend as well as to stretch.'

LIN CHUNG *pauses in deep thought*
This is good. In view of what you say, let's go!

LU CHYAN *greatly pleased*
Now you're making sense.

LIN CHUNG *sings*
With sword in hand
I go out the gate.

LU CHYAN Virtuous Brother, after you.

LIN CHUNG *and* LU CHYAN *mime exiting from the house into the street;* LIN SHOU *mimes closing the gate, exits*

Enter LU JR SHEN

LU JR SHEN Ah, Virtuous Brother! *Continues the singing*
Just *where* are you going?

LIN CHUNG *stops* LU CHYAN

Elder Brother has been waiting a long time for you in the vegetable garden – where are you going?

LIN CHUNG Benevolent Brother, there is something you don't know; the fact that I bought a precious sword came to be known to the Minister of War; he ordered Little Brother to bring the sword to his home, that he may look at it.

LU JR SHEN *puzzled*
Ai! For no reason at all he wants to look at the sword? Virtuous Brother, don't go! Quickly, let's go to the vegetable garden and drink! *He tries to pull* LIN CHUNG *away*

LU CHYAN *wonders out loud*
Virtuous Brother?

LIN CHUNG Ah, Benevolent Brother, here is Brother Lu who has come to ask me to go with *him!* How is it possible for me not to go?

To LU CHYAN

Ah! Brother Lu, I am tied as blood brother to Benevolent Brother Lu. Come meet each other.

LU CHYAN Hm, hm, hm. Virtuous Brother Lin and I are classmates of the School of Military Arts. Truly, we're as close as hand and foot. This is a Minister of War's invitation; how can it be proper *not* to go! After this matter is taken care of, I'll go together with Virtuous Brother Lin to the vegetable garden, and visit you, Master Lu.

LU JR SHEN Mm . . .

LIN CHUNG That's right. Brother Lu is my life-and-death old friend. *Points to* LU CHYAN Together we go, and together we come back. In a short time we'll be at the vegetable garden to drink with you.

LU CHYAN That's right; that's right.

LU JR SHEN Very well, very well. Virtuous Brother, go quickly. But return at once: My invitation stands that you drink with me in the vegetable garden.

LIN CHUNG So, Brother, you and I will part from each other temporarily.

LU JR SHEN Temporarily, we'll part.

LIN CHUNG *sings*
Let's raise our hands in farewell
Before starting our journey.
Please, go first.

Exit LIN CHUNG *and* LU CHYAN

LU JR SHEN *suddenly alarmed*
Ah!

Sings

I turn aside, to think to myself;
If Virtuous Brother returns, there's nothing
　　　to say or do;

If mischance befalls him,
There I'll go and raise Hell.
No matter what soldiers or generals,
I vow that they'll die one by one,
Like ghosts with their tongues hanging out!
I turn toward the vegetable garden
And take my leave.
I'll lead my men to seek out each truth!

Exits

SCENE 8   *White Tiger Hall. A large painting of a tiger is upstage center,*
indicating the locale. GAU SHR DE, FU AN *enter, whisper to each*
other. They call up eight prison guards, whisper to them. All
exit

LIN CHUNG *enters, sings*
On the way, I think, I hesitate,
I'm in conflict with myself.

I enter into the big hall and gallery.

LU CHYAN   Virtuous Brother, please enter.

VOICE
OFFSTAGE   The Minister of War is not at the back hall; he orders Lin Chung
to the second hall to confer.

LIN CHUNG   Ah!

Sings

The Minister of War bids me
To present myself in the second hall

Turns to LU CHYAN

May I trouble you, Brother Lu, to go with me?

LU CHYAN, LIN CHUNG *walk about the stage*

LU CHYAN *sings*
I do not see where the War Minister is.
Come, come, come!
Follow me to the study!

Virtuous Brother

Virtuous Brother, wait a moment,
And don't be worried.

Virtuous Brother, wait a moment here; wait for me to enter within to pass the word for you. *Exits*

LIN CHUNG *enters the great hall, looks about*
I see that the hall is still. Wu hu ya! The atmosphere is awesome. I wonder what this place is? *He sees the sign,* White Tiger Hall Ai, ya! Let me stop and think! This is White Tiger Hall, and I believe a place for confidential military talks; without cause, how is it possible to gain entrance to this important place? Let me turn and leave!

Sings

At once I turn and go.

VOICE
OFFSTAGE Catch the killer!

Eight prison guards enter and take hold of LIN CHUNG

GUARDS Report to the Minister of War! A killer is caught!

Eight more guards and GAU CHYOU ENTER

GAU CHYOU *sits*
Bring the prisoner before me.

GUARDS Bring forth the prisoner

Eight prison guards grab LIN CHUNG, *making him kneel before* GAU CHYOU

GAU CHYOU *stares at* LIN CHUNG
Tu! What gall, Lin Chung, to sneak into White Tiger Hall bearing a sword to kill me! Who set you on me? Still you won't speak?

LIN CHUNG I'm here, simply because Lu Chyan, following your order, called me to this place. Please seek the truth.

GAU CHYOU *enraged*
Shut up! How did I bid you come here? Oh, ho, so this is it: I've heard that for many days now you've concealed a sharp sword on your person; lying in wait for me outside my gate. Today with this sword you sneaked into the military strategy hall, obviously to kill me. Don't tell me you dare contradict me! What else do you have to say for yourself?

LIN CHUNG *calm and with conviction*
Minister of War, if you do not believe this, please call for Nobleman Lu to come here. Once you've asked him, all will be cleared up.

GAU CHYOU *pretends to agree*
Hm! I do want to clear this up –

To guards

Come –

GUARDS Present.

GAU CHYOU Ask Lu Chyan to come forth.

GUARD Ask Lu Chyan to come forth.

LU CHYAN *enters*

LU CHYAN My respects to the Minister of War.

GAU CHYOU *angrily*
Lu Chyan! Lin Chung entered White Tiger Hall and tried to kill me. Was it you who brought him to this place? Speak up, speak!

LU CHYAN *calmly, as if nothing happened*
Minister of War, please suppress your anger. Even though I am ignorant, I know what is right and what is wrong; furthermore your kindnesses reach to the mountains, and I have no way to repay them. How could I have plotted with him to come here to kill you. Please, seek the truth! Minister of War.

GAU CHYOU Lin Chung, what do you have to say?

LIN CHUNG *failing to suppress his anger longer, he turns to* LU CHYAN
Brother Lu!

LU CHYAN Oh, Drillmaster Lin.

LIN CHUNG By order of the Minister of War, you asked me to come here. Why don't you speak up?

LU CHYAN *with deceit*
As for the Minister of War's orders, I don't know anything about them.

LIN CHUNG You asked me to bring the sword here to show it to the Minister of War, didn't you?

LU CHYAN What sword? Contrary to what you're saying, it's not clear at all.

LIN CHUNG *in extreme anger*
Wasn't it *indeed* you who guided me falsely into White Tiger Hall?

LU CHYAN Drillmaster, don't wrong me deliberately. You say that it was I, who guided you here! What proof do you have? Who's the witness? Furthermore, from this morning I didn't leave the side of the Minister of War. The Minister is my witness. Drillmaster Lin, I advise you: Tell the truth about what you did! Why drag me into it? If you insist on being guiltless, it won't help the matter to accuse wrongly an innocent man!

GAU CHYOU   Seemingly you are involving an innocent man? Guards!

GUARDS   Present

GAU CHYOU   Take him away. Have him beheaded.

LIN CHUNG   I am accused wrongly!

GAU CHYOU   Lin Chung, we have here witnesses in evidence. And, you still claim you're wrongly accused.

LIN CHUNG   *angrily*
Minister of War, let me say something.

GAU CHYOU   Speak.

LIN CHUNG   I am a rough, clumsy military man, but I quite know the laws, the difference between right and wrong. How could I without leave enter White Tiger Hall? I cite the past: on the twenty-eighth day of the fourth month, my wife went to the Dung Ywe Temple to burn incense, fulfilling her obligation to a vow; while walking up to the temple, by chance, she met your son and Lu Chyan; in a hundred different ways your son made advances to *my* wife. I rushed there. With hue and cry, I was able to make them go away. Concerning *this* whole matter, *I* have witnesses. Later, by chance I bought a precious sword. In the same way fell I into the trap laid by the villain selling the sword, so was I fooled into entering the White Tiger Hall. The Minister of War comes here, not allowing me to defend myself, saying that with sword in hand I plan to kill him. I hope the Minister of War holds high the mirror of justice, restoring the purity of my innocence.

GAU CHYOU   *Furious*
Unh . . . What a smooth speaker!

LIN CHUNG   Each word I said was true.

GAU CHYOU   Ya, ya, pei! Granted, my son is young. But from an early age, he studied poetry and literature. He has a tender conscience. How is it possible for him to have made advances to your wife? Obviously you're trying to slander him. Am I to permit that? Guards!

GUARDS   Present.

GAU CHYOU   Eighty heavy lashes. Beat him.

Guards answer, push LIN CHUNG *down, and start to beat him*

GUARDS   Ten, twenty, thirty, forty, fifty, sixty, seventy, eighty – the beating is done.

GAU CHYOU   Lin Chung, still you don't confess?

LIN CHUNG   *sings, showing pain*
Beaten with eighty lashes,
My anger and hatred rush to the sky!

Continues singing

So beaten
That my skin and flesh split open
And my blood flows.
Absolutely unknowingly by Lu, the thief,
Was I led into the trap;
Now where may I go
To clear away this injustice!
Today, how difficult it seems
To escape and to stay alive.

LU CHYAN   *malevolently*
Drillmaster Lin, how about confessing!

LIN CHUNG   *spitting*
Pei!

Continues to sing

I'd rather die than confess!

GAU CHYOU Do you or don't you confess?

They torture LIN CHUNG *again, he faints.* GAU CHYOU *orders them to revive him with water*

LIN CHUNG Nothing to confess!

GAU CHYOU Shackle him, take him to jail; clear the hall!

GUARDS Yes.
Eight prison guards exit with LIN CHUNG

GAU CHYOU *rising*
Lin Chung would not confess. What other ideas do you have to get rid of him.

LU CHYAN *maliciously*
I have a plot which serves two goals.

GAU CHYOU Speak.

LU CHYAN Yes, I see that whether Lin Chung confesses or not, it's not important. First, let us consider his crime for entering the military strategy room, wearing a sword, and attempting to kill the Minister of War. By law he would have been sentenced to death, but because of the Minister of War's benevolence, punishment for the crime is reduced. Turn him over to the authorities of Kai Feng city, for exile to Tsang Jou! Then with silver I'll bribe the guards to take him half way and kill him. When Lin Chung's wife has word of Lin Chung's death, she'll be without hope. Then you order someone to go to her and propose marriage. Your son's marriage must succeed. Would that not serve two goals?

GAU CHYOU Follow up this scheme, carry it out! Go!

LU CHYAN I obey your command.

All exit

SCENE 9   *On the road to Kai Feng. Performed before an act curtain*

JANG YUNG Oh, in my heart,
How I am enraged by the thief, Gau Chyou:
To entrap a virtuous scholar
Through schemes and plots.
I walk to the rear of the Long Pavilion;
When my virtuous son-in-law arrives,
I'll ask him to explain all.

Enter GUARDS *and* LIN CHUNG. LIN CHUNG *wears a cangue, a board imprisoning his neck and hands. On his face is a gold-colored brand, indicating he is a prisoner*

GUARDS Move on!

LIN CHUNG *sings*
As a fierce tiger falls into a cage,
I fell into the hands of thieves.
Oh, for the day that I may avenge myself;
Now I suppress my anger
And swallow the sound.
I walk toward the Long Pavilion.

SYWE BA (GUARD *in charge of* LIN CHUNG)
Lin Chung, stop this nonsense and hurry up! If you stall, I'll hit you.

DUNG CHAU (GUARD *in charge of* LIN CHUNG) *spits*
Pei! Pei! Go quickly.

LIN CHUNG Oh! Officer!

SYWE BA *as the father-in-law approaches*
Hey there! I ask you: what are you up to?

JANG YUNG I, an old man, am Jang Yung.

SYWE BA I didn't ask you that. What are you doing here?

JANG YUNG Oh, I've come to see my son-in-law here.

SYWE BA Oh, so I see you are Lin Chung's old father-in-law. This is a misfortune that has befallen your family. You meet us so politely! *But* if I were so polite to you, then you'd take advantage! I tell you: this is official business. You are not allowed to meet him.

JANG YUNG Guard, just this once make it possible for me to talk to him.

He bows, raising his clasped hands to his forehead

SYWE BA It's a pity that you, in your advanced years, still don't understand anything!

JANG YUNG Ah, Master Guard, here's for a cup of tea.* *Starts to give him the silver* Go have a drink on me.

SYWE BA Step out of the way! *Takes the silver and smiles. To fellow* GUARD Well – hey, yey! As a matter of fact, it doesn't matter that they see and talk to each other. Fellow, isn't that right? Letting them meet a bit, it doesn't matter?

DUNG CHAU What?

SYWE BA It doesn't matter!

DUNG CHAU It doesn't matter? What you said doesn't count. Business should be managed in a businesslike way. Before it's too late, you'd better make him beat it!

* This is a euphemism in Chinese for giving him a bribe, much exceeding the cost of a cup of tea, of course.

SYWE BA Fellow, we're friends, isn't that true?

DUNG CHAU Friends? I don't understand what you call friendship, I don't understand, don't understand.

SYWE BA *to father-in-law*
Who do you think you are? Well, Old Man, I'm easy, the only thing is: my fellow guard doesn't understand 'friendship.' *You* go over there and speak to him. I'm out of it. *He steps aside*

JANG YUNG *to* PUNG CHAU
Ah, Officer, I've come here to see my son-in-law. Officer, give us a break. *He bows with clasped hands to forehead*

DUNG CHAU Friendship? I don't understand it but business is easy: you people want to talk? It doesn't matter.

JANG YUNG Officer, please get yourself some tea. *Gives him the silver*

DUNG CHAU Hmm. See, business is easy to manage. We, like father and son, are friends. *To* SYWE BA Fellow, take off the cangue.

SYWE BA *removes the cangue*

JANG YUNG *sings*
Seeing Virtuous Son wearing the badge of crime,
My heart is troubled.

LIN CHUNG *continues the singing*
I hope Father-in-Law forgives,
Son-in-Law's manners being improper.

JANG YUNG Son-in-Law is exiled to Tsang Jou! Once my daughter heard the news, she prepared herself, and is coming to the Long Pavilion to meet you. I hope that Virtuous Son-in-Law will wait for just a while!

LIN CHUNG Hmm, fine, fine, fine! I have one matter to discuss with you, Father-in-Law.

JANG YUNG Virtuous Son-in-Law, please speak.

LIN CHUNG   As I think of being entrapped by the traitor – and being exiled to Tsang Jou; I realize that after I leave, I leave behind at home my delicate wife. Do you think that that thief in the Gau family will let it go at that?

JANG YUNG   Ai, ya, Virtuous Son-in-Law! True, today you go into exile to Tsang Jou. But in all family matters, you have me to shoulder them. If that thief doesn't come to molest me, then all is well; but if he so much as behaves rudely toward my daughter, then I will face him, fighting to the end, without caring a pin for my life.

LIN CHUNG   Father-in-Law! I am honored by your daring, but what a pity that the Gau family's official power is so hard to resist. *Sighs* What to do? That's the way things are – I must confess to you last night I had written down a writ of annulment, giving up your daughter, bidding her to remarry if she wishes. I would not stand in the way; from now on, I, Lin Chung, may have peace of mind.

JANG YUNG   By all means, don't do it.

LIN CHUNG   *sings*
In the jail I finished the writ of annulment,
To cut the love relationship between husband and wife.

He takes out the writ

Letting each go a separate way.
I present the writ
And hurriedly kneel before you.

LIN CHUNG *kneels;* JANG YUNG *goes to his side*

JANG YUNG   *continues the singing and lifts* LIN CHUNG
I beg that Virtuous Son-in-Law
Will stop his sad tears.
Don't be anxious!

LADY JANG *enters with* JIN ER. *Seeing* LIN CHUNG, LADY JANG *kneels*

LADY JANG *sings*
>   Seeing my husband,
>   I cannot help shedding tears;
>   Ten thousand knives pierce my heart.
>   How pitiable; you've been wronged.
>   You – have been tricked!
>   How I had hoped
>   You and I, husband and wife
>   Would reach old age together.

She cries loudly, and rises

>   Never had I thought
>   That all in one second,
>   We'd be separated!
>   Each going his own way!

Husband, ah, how hateful that a villainous thief set up a venomous plot to entrap us; we, one flesh and blood, separated; without cause, to exile you to Tsang Jou. Today, as you go upon the road; take much, much care of yourself. After this has passed, you must come back soon! So husband and wife will be reunited. Husband! What several words do you have to advise your wife?

LIN CHUNG *declaiming in a wailing or crying tone*
>   Wife, ah!
>   I, Lin Chung, entrapped by villainous traitors
>   Have dragged you, an innocent wife, into the mud.
>   You have met misfortune.
>   After I'm gone,
>   I hope that Virtuous Wife will be patient in all things,
>   Taking every care;
>   You . . . from this day forth,
>   Don't think of me.

LADY JANG Husband why do you say such things?

LIN CHUNG *recites*
>   Lovebirds flying together with matched wings,
>   Suddenly are swept away by the tide, separated.

Tidal waves beat the Mandarin ducks,
Sending each in a different direction.

Cries and sings

I counsel, Virtuous wife,
That you let not your tears fall.
Don't think of me
As a heartless person!
– Supposing the Gau family thieves
Plot once again.

LADY JANG *continues the singing*
Your wife will fight them to the death.

LIN CHUNG *sings*
Were I to meet with misfortune on the way,
Lose my life –

LADY JANG *continues*
I would wear hempen garments and a black band for you.
I would spend the rest of my life alone.

LIN CHUNG *continues the singing*
With thousands and thousands of words
I tell you but you understand not:
I have no choice but to choose.

He takes out the writ

I hope Dear Wife, you will forgive me –

He starts to give his wife the writ, but changes his mind

For not looking after you.

DUNG CHAU Hey!

Continues the singing

When you two started to sing,

There was no end of it.
That won't do.

JIN ER *hands some clothing and some silver to* SYWE BA, *who gives
the clothes to* DUNG CHAU, *but puts the silver in his own pocket*

You've got to leave.

LIN CHUNG *sings*
    Eyes with flowing tears
    Look to eyes with flowing tears;
    One who is heartbroken
    Parts from one who is heartbroken.

SYWE BA
AND
DUNG CHAU *in unison*

Leave, leave, leave!

LIN CHUNG *looking at the writ, finally makes up his mind, rushes
to* LADY JANG, *grabs her hand*

Oh, Wife, you have to take care now! *Gives her the writ*

The two guards pull at LIN CHUNG *and begin to walk away.*
LADY JANG *reads the writ*

LADY JANG Ai, ya! *She tears the writ and faints*

LIN CHUNG Ai, ya! Oh, Wife, oh, Wife, oh, Wife! *He kneels to* LADY JANG.
Two guards pull him away, beating him

LADY JANG *sings*
    My mind is upset.
    Jin Er – Husband, Husband!

All exit

SCENE 10 *On the road. An evening-sky backdrop and a row of bushes comprise the scenery.* LU JR SHEN *enters, carrying a staff. He circles the stage to indicate running*

LU JR SHEN How maddening!
My followers came and reported!
My rage grows, my rage grows!
Virtuous Brother, has met with foul play.
Hurriedly I run ahead;
In an instant I'll reach the Wild Boar Forest.

Hold it! My Virtuous Brother Lin Chung, tricked by villainous Gau Chyou, the thief, is now sent into exile to Tsang Jou. Definitely he'll pass by here. How right for me to hide myself inside the wood to rescue Virtuous Brother. So be it. *Exits*

LIN CHUNG *sings offstage*
All the way, beaten by unfeeling clubs,
Truly it's hard to bear any longer.

Enter LIN CHUNG *and two guards who are beating him*

DUNG CHAU Let's go!

LIN CHUNG *continuing to sing*
I have been tricked, falsely accused;
To whom do I turn to clear my name?
Now, under an inhuman sentence,
I carry chains, wear the cangue!
Even had I wings
It would be difficult to rise.

With each line of singing, LIN CHUNG *is given a whack by a guard*

SYWE BA
AND
DUNG CHAU Go on! Go on!

LIN CHUNG *continues to sing*
A villainous thief works things out too cruelly;
Entrapping us, Husband and Wife:

So we are separated in different directions!
At the Long Pavilion I divorced my wife.
It is difficult to bring our words to an end;
It's like steel knives, stabbing my heart.
Now my only wish is
That my wife be safe,
Escaping harm.

Continues singing

– Two guards,
Carrying out orders,
Abuse me!

DUNG CHAU
    AND
  SYWE BA Get on quickly!

LIN CHUNG *singing*
I bid you stop and forego your cruelty;
Who has not heard of me,
Drillmaster of eight hundred thousand Imperial Guards!
I can hold back my anger no longer!
How difficult to swallow hatred . . .

Lin Chung starts to attack the guards

DUNG CHAU
    AND
  SYWE BA Ai ya, Drillmaster Lin, Spare our lives!

LIN CHUNG Let's see now
If you still dare to behave badly!

DUNG CHAU Why are you so angry with us! You're very tired, go there and rest a moment.

SYWE BA Drillmaster Lin, you are tired from walking. Before we set out again, rest a moment.

DUNG CHAU   Drillmaster Lin, over there's a big tree. Go and rest a bit.

SYWE BA   Drillmaster Lin, rest a moment. Rest a moment! We, Brothers, will also rest. – Ah, once we've rested enough, then we'll set out again. By this tree, rest a bit. Take it easy, sitting down.

Lin Chung sits down apart

DUNG CHAU   *whispers to* SYWE BA
Ai! Oh my Grandmother! * This job is not easy to carry out, but we're stuck with it.

SYWE BA   Have you figured it out?

DUNG CHAU   A long time ago I figured it out. We're stuck with it! What to do about it, fellow?

SYWE BA   I have an idea: let's just wait and when he least expects it, suddenly we'll tie him to the tree, take his sword, kill him dead! Reporting back to Minister Gau, each of us'll claim the two hundred ounces of silver. How does that strike you?

DUNG CHAU   Good idea!

They attack LIN CHUNG, *tying him to the tree*

LIN CHUNG   Ah! What's the meaning of this?

DUNG CHAU   What's the meaning of this? Just look at this sword! *Here* is your enemy. Minister Gau gives the two of us brothers each two hundred ounces of silver each, bidding us on the way kill you dead! Now after you're dead, don't blame us, the two of us, for being vile and poisonous.

LIN CHUNG   Ai ya! You two fellows, do you mean to tell me you've listened to and believed the words of a Gau Chyou, and intend to harm me?

* The Chinese is the equivalent to the Western curse, 'My God' or 'Jesus Christ.'

SYWE BA
AND
DUNG CHAU   Shut up! If the Minister of War orders you die on the third hour, how can we spare you until the fifth hour?

They sing

I raise the steel sword,
I take your life.

LU JR SHEN *appears from behind the tree; with his staff he knocks down the two guards.*

LU JR SHEN   *continues the singing*
Fearless dog's head,
To dare to harm this man!
How dare you risk harming my blood brother!

DUNG CHAU
AND
SYWE BA   We didn't . . .

LIN CHUNG   How about forgiving them!

LU JR SHEN   Without doubt, these two dog heads intended to kill you, Virtuous Brother! Why do you ask favors for them? *Spits* Pei! I'll kill them . . .

LIN CHUNG   Behind any wrongs is *one* man: just as debts take you to the lender, go directly to the man behind the plot. Why argue with *these* two rats!

LU JR SHEN   All right, for your sake, Virtuous Brother, then I spare them.

DUNG CHAU
AND
SYWE BA   *bowing*
Many thanks to you, Old Buddha, for sparing our lives!

LU JR SHEN   Quickly release Drillmaster Lin!

DUNG CHAU
AND
SYWE BA   Yes, yes. Let me do it! Let me do it!
            Ai ya, Drillmaster Lin. Ah, our sincere apologies to you; we let
            you suffer unjustly. *They rub his back and his feet*

LU JR SHEN Beat it. Go over there! *Guards withdraw to the side, and face the
            audience* Kneel down! *Turning to* LIN CHUNG

            Virtuous Brother!

LIN CHUNG   Benevolent Brother, how was it possible for you to get here, to
            rescue Little Brother?

LU JR SHEN Ever since you went away, Virtuous Brother, my heart was ill at
            ease; so I ordered my followers to ask for news of Virtuous
            Brother. I know that you had been entrapped by Gau Chyou,
            sent into exile to Tsang Jou. So I came to rescue you.

LIN CHUNG   Oh, now I see!

LU JR SHEN Virtuous Brother, follow me quickly and return to the Eastern
            Capital; first we'll kill Gau Chyou dead, then jubilantly break up
            the place!

LIN CHUNG   *in agreement*
            Humph! Benevolent Brother, for the time being, let's go to
            Tsang Jou; then decide what to do.

LU JR SHEN Fine, Foolish Brother will protect you straight to Tsang Jou.
            What do you think of that?

LIN CHUNG   What you say is very good. Let's leave! *Feels unbearable pain*

LU JR SHEN Virtuous Brother, what's the matter?

LIN CHUNG   I have sores all over my body; I'm not able to walk.

LU JR SHEN Well . . . What to do! Hmm. *Thinking – turns, sees the guards,
            and gets an idea* Now I have it, now I have it! *Calls contemp-
            tuously* Te! What are you called?

DUNG CHAU *and* SYWE BA *face* LU JR SHEN

DUNG CHAU   What's my name, now I . . . have forgotten it! Eh, Eh, now I remember it; I'm called Dung Chau.

LU JR SHEN   What about you?

SYWE BA   I'm called Sywe Ba.

LU JR SHEN   Dung Chau, Sywe Ba.

DUNG CHAU
AND
SYWE BA   *in unison*
Here!

LU JR SHEN   I command the two of you.

DUNG CHAU
AND
SYWE BA   Present.

LU JR SHEN   Look after Drillmaster Lin.

DUNG CHAU
AND
SYWE BA   Yes!

LU JR SHEN   Straight to Tsang Jou . . .

DUNG CHAU
AND
SYWE BA   Yes!

LU JR SHEN   All the way . . .

DUNG CHAU
AND
SYWE BA   Yes!

LU JR SHEN Take turns carrying him on your shoulders.

DUNG CHAU
AND
SYWE BA Yes!

LU JR SHEN But if a very little thing goes wrong: Hmmm, hmm . . .

DUNG CHAU
AND
SYWE BA Oh, My Mother! *They crawl on the ground*

LU JR SHEN I'll certainly take the lives of you two dogs!

DUNG CHAU
AND
SYWE BA Yes, Old Buddha. *They bow*

LU JR SHEN Quick, let's go!

DUNG CHAU
AND
SYWE BA Yes! *They rise*

SYWE BA I'll carry him.

DUNG CHAU *I* will carry him.

SYWE BA *I* will carry him. *Pushes* DUNG CHAU

DUNG CHAU *I* will carry him. *Pushes* SYWE BA

LU JR SHEN Stop carrying on so!

DUNG CHAU Take it easy, take it easy! Don't get panicky and I'll not hurry either. Look, I've an idea! Ask Master Lin to sit in a sedan chair. *He gestures with his hands, suggesting how the two will carry him, with locked arms*

SYWE BA Right.

DUNG CHAU
    AND
SYWE BA *in unison*
Invite Drillmaster Lin to sit in a sedan chair. Up! *They lift him with locked hands* Old Buddha, how goes it?

LU JR SHEN Not bad. Quick, let's go!

DUNG CHAU
    AND
SYWE BA Let's go!

Guards exit, carrying LIN CHUNG, *followed by* LU JR SHEN

SCENE 11 *Residence of* LADY JANG's *father* JANG YUNG

Lady Jang enters, assisted by her maid, JIN ER

LADY JANG *sings*
Ever since that day I parted from my husband,
I have been gravely ill.
I have no strength at all,
It's as though I have lost three souls.
Thinking of the past, my heart breaks
And I cannot stop my tears falling.

She sits

I hope that my husband will come back home very soon.

JANG YUNG *continues singing*
Unfortunately, my daughter is ill;
Before one trouble ends, another one comes.

He mimes entering by the door to his daughter's room

My daughter, how do you feel today?

LADY JANG Slightly recovered. My father, have you heard anything of my husband's whereabouts?

JANG YUNG Your father went into the street to inquire; and somebody said that your husband had already arrived at Tsang Jou. He will be able to come back before long.

LADY JANG I wish that my husband would escape out of the hands of the thieves and stay alive. Even if I were to die under the Nine Springs, then I would have no complaints.* *She cries, then sings*
I hope that my husband stays alive.
Then even if I die under the Nine Springs,
I will be at peace.

GAU SHR DE *offstage, sings*
I came out of my door and the air is full of happiness.

Four servants, two sedan chair carriers, TAU FU, FU AN, *and* GAU SHR DE *enter*

GAU SHR DE *continues the singing*
I am the groom, marrying a bride.
I had my hair cut, bathed, and changed into new clothes.
Happiness has come to my door,
I am being mated with a phoenix.†
Tonight I'll enter the bridal chamber.
The Old Man in the moon pairs us together.

Hai! Keep walking.

FU AN Don't walk farther; we are already there.

GAU SHR DE Oh! We're already there! *Looks about* That's not right. But this is not Lin Chung's home.

---

* The Chinese expression *Nine Springs* means a worthless, horrible death.
† The term phoenix in China has been used to describe an elegant, regal lady.

FU AN   You didn't know! After Lin Chung left, she moved back to live in her father's house.

GAU SHR DE   Oh, this is the home of the father-in-law. Good. I will go to knock on the door. *He fixes his appearance, smooths down his robe. Uses a high-pitched voice* Oh, Father-in-Law, please come and open the door.

> JANG YUNG *upstage,* LADY JANG, *and* JIN ER *start at hearing the voice.* JANG YUNG *motions with a glance, that* LADY JANG *and* JIN ER *exit*

> *With a sword in hand,* JANG YUNG *mimes opening the door*

JANG YUNG   Who is this? *With anger, he stands erect*

GAU SHR DE   *with surprise*
You! How is it that there comes an executioner? I see this man is full of bravado, and an awesome air. I wonder who this person is?

FU AN   This is the father-in-law.

GAU SHR DE   Ai ya! My Father-in-Law is so brave and heroic looking that I can only use the word formidable to describe him.

FU AN   He has come with a sword. You'd better be careful.

GAU SHR DE   Never mind, never mind. I know what I am doing. *He walks toward* JANG YUNG Ah! My elder, here I am paying my respects.

JANG YUNG   Here are *my* respects. *Shows sword*

GAU SHR DE   May I ask you, my elder, what your name is! Where are you from? What do you do for a living? And how old you are?

JANG YUNG   This old man is Jang Yung.

GAU SHR DE   Ai ya, ya! I have long heard that name and just like 'five peals of thunder blasting the tops.' *

* He is mangling the phrase, 'His name is thunder to the ears.'

FU AN What was that? You mean: 'Great thunder fills the ear with your fame.'

GAU SHR DE Oh yes, 'Great thunder fills the ears' . . . Now that I see you, I truly can not say much about you.*

FU AN What?

GAU SHR DE Oh! Now that I see you, indeed it is . . . 'I bend in order to make a sacrifice.'

FU AN No, you mean, 'The reports I have had of you do not lie.'

GAU SHR DE Oh, otherwise . . . 'ah, . . . sure enough . . . therefore . . . once for all . . . , I'm flattered, I'm flattered.'

JANG YUNG Who are you?

GAU SHR DE My name is Gau; I am called Shr De. I am the son of the current War Minister.

JANG YUNG Hmmp! What are you doing here?

GAU SHR DE Simply because Lin Chung, who had committed a serious crime, was exiled to Tsang Jyou, and lost his life on the way, I think that your daughter who at such a young age stays in the empty bedroom, is wasting of her youth. I intend to climb the ladder to marry your daughter. Such a couple can truly be called as 'The groom is talented and the bride is beautiful.' It's truly 'made in heaven, and live to be a hundred years old.' 'Enjoy the life of heaven on earth.' Look, look, look, Father-in-Law, 'Please look at me, your son-in-law: I have eyes, long eyebrows, straight nose, and square mouth. She is beautiful, but unpretentious.' This is what I have to say. So dear Father-in-law, Please accept my bow. *He is ready to bow*

JANG YUNG *slaps* GAU's *face*
What a thief!

FU AN, *seeing this, runs offstage*

* Meant as a compliment, it comes out as an insult.

GAU SHR DE   Ha! Ha! You violent man, how primitive; right on top of a conversation, you can't utter good words and you slap people besides. I would call this 'blah, blah, blah, blah!' I'm not going to take this any longer. Old 'rabbit lantern.' You are trying to make me lose face! You . . . 'Grandson!' *

JANG YUNG   Enough! You son of a dog! Leaning on your father's influence, you behave recklessly, oppressing the good and snatching the wife of a citizen. Now because of you, the family of Lin Chung has been torn apart. I can't wait to cut you in tens of hundreds of pieces. Only then my mind's hatred will be at ease.

Sings

Raising my steel sword
I'm taking your life!

Grabs GAU SHR DE, *ready to kill him. Four* GAU CHYOU *house guards come forward to shove* JANG YUNG; *but* JANG YUNG *subdues them. They exit*

FU AN   *enters with eight guards.* They tie up JANG YUNG *and exit with him;* JIN ER, *the maid, enters running, sees the situation and hurriedly exits*

FU AN *and* GAU FU *help* GAU SHR DE *up*

FU AN   My Lord, my Lord!

GAU SHR DE   Ai Ya! Ai Ya! Where is my head?

FU AN   Your head is still where it was.

GAU SHR DE   *feels his head*
Really? Ai, isn't it a fact that it didn't move? Ai Ya. What a near miss. That great chaos a while ago: what was it all about?

FU AN   Didn't you know? When I saw that old man Jang acting funny, I hurriedly went back – dispatched some guards and chained him up in the court. This is what it's all about.

* Used in Chinese as a humiliating epithet.

GAU SHR DE Ai Ya, So, I'm indebted to you for my life, just as I am to my parents.

FU AN You flatter me! You flatter me!

GAU SHR DE What should I do now?

FU AN There's nobody home just now; you should hurry in to finish the marriage.

GAU SHR DE Right, let's go get the marriage over.

GAU SHR DE is ready to leave; FU AN, GAU FU, *start to follow*

GAU SHR DE Hey! Hey! Why are you two going?

FU AN To protect your lordship at the wedding.

GAU SHR DE Now I don't need anybody to protect me. Get out in the hall, and be ready to serve.

FU AN Yes.

FU AN, GAU FU *exit* LADY JANG *enters, assisted by* JIN ER

LADY JANG *sings*
Jin Er, quickly, find out
What has happened for me!

She mimes crossing a threshold to enter the room. She bumps into GAU SHR DE, *who is trying to enter her room*

GAU SHR DE *uses a tender high-pitched voice*
Ah, My Lady.

Sings falsetto voice of Clown Chou

Please forgive my intrusion, my lady;
How do you feel?

Ah, my Lady, ever since that day when I saw your face, I have not been wanting to drink any tea or eat any food. So, hurry up, and follow me: to live in luxury and to enjoy wealth . . . Ah, my Lady! I presume that you are not going to refuse . . . ha, ha, ha . . .

LADY JANG   Stop it! You and others had set up a venomous plot, which caused my family all to be separated. You wait until my husband comes back; he'll never let you get away with it!

GAU SHR DE   Forget it! Your husband has been killed on the road! He can't come back anymore!

LADY JANG   You . . . is what you said true?

GAU SHR DE   If I deceive you, I am not a human being.

LADY JANG   *wailing*
Wei Ya! My husband!

GAU SHR DE   *mimics her*
Wei Ya! My wife!

JIN ER   Get out! *Slaps* GAU SHR DE'*s face* My Lady, don't cry just now! Let's kill this runt.*

GAU SHR DE   You! This little wench! How dare you hit me?

LADY JANG *and* JIN ER *each take out a dagger, and chase* GAU SHR DE, *trying to stab him.* JIN ER *closes the door,* LADY JANG *stabs* GAU SHR DE *in the leg, wounding him.* GAU SHR DE *grabs* JIN ER'*s knife and, stabbing her, kills her. He feels pain in his leg, falls down.*

LADY JANG   Wei Ya

Sings

* Literally 'little one,' a phrase of contempt, *syau dz.*

I open my eyes and see my family dying, one by one,
Leaving me all by myself: why should I live on this cold world?
I bite my teeth: I'll fight to the death this sneak.

LADY JANG *stabs* GAU SHR DE *again; he faints.* GAU SHR DE *stabs*
LADY JANG *in the leg.*

LADY JANG Wei Ya!

Sings

I am but a frail and helpless woman,
My strength is not equal to him.
It is difficult to overcome him.
I am wondering whether my husband is really dead.

My husband! My husband! Are you really dead?

Sings

There's no answer to my wailing,
And I do not know whether he's alive or dead;
Now, it's getting very difficult for me
To endure the pain in my leg;
Blood rushes to my head.

Enough!

Sings

I am ready to rend the web of love and life
And consider it all a dream!

LADY JANG *cuts her throat and dies*

GAU SHR DE Ai you! Don't die! Don't die! Ai you! *Cries*

Wa . . .

FU AN, GAU FU *enter with four house guards*

FU AN How is it that they still haven't come out? Ya! The door is still closed. Your lordship! Your lordship!

GAU SHR DE *moaning*
Ai! . . .

FU AN Open the door! Open the door!

GAU SHR DE I can't! Kick it!

FU AN Yes! Kick the door!

The crowd mimes kicking the door and then they enter

My God! How come everybody's dead?

GAU SHR DE Hurry up and get me up!

FU AN *lifting* GAU SHR DE
What has happened to you?

GAU SHR DE Ai! Ai! I was stabbed by the little wench, and it hit me right at my hemorrhoids. The little wench did it; she stabbed me in the hemorrhoids!

FU AN You! How come it stinks so here?

GAU SHR DE Don't you people shout. Now my bowel movements will be easy! Let's go home!

The crowd, assisting GAU SHR DE, *exits*

SCENE 12 GAU CHYOU's *home*

SYWE BA *You* go a little faster.

DUNG CHAU Ai, old fellow, will it do, if we say it like that? How can we tell them?

SYWE BA   If you don't say it that way, then how else will you say it.

DUNG CHAU   We've not handled this thing well, at all, Old Fellow!

SYWE BA   So it wasn't done well! We didn't want to do it!

DUNG CHAU   Now for the silver, do we or don't we still ask for it?

SYWE BA   If they give it to us, then we take it, if not, then we forget about it!

DUNG CHAU   If it's *not* given, then we forget about it?

SYWE BA   Nothing will go wrong! You listen to what I say.

DUNG CHAU   I'll listen to what you say.

SYWE BA   When we get there, whatever I say, you say the same.

DUNG CHAU   Right! Whatever you say, I'll say. Let's get going!

SYWE BA   Stop! We're there . . . Is someone at the gate?

JUNG JUN   What do you want?

SYWE BA   Can I ask: is Nobleman Lu within?

JUNG JUN   Where do you come from?

SYWE BA   We're from Kaifeng: Dung Chau and Sywe Ba seek an audience.

JUNG JUN   Just wait . . . There is a request for Nobleman Lu.

LU CHYAN *enters*

LU CHYAN   What's the matter?

JUNG JUN   Dung Chau and Sywe Ba from the Kaifeng seek an audience.

LU CHYAN   Let them enter.

JUNG JUN   It shall be – from within the request is granted – take care!

SYWE BA *to* DUNG CHAU

Yes – let's go in, let's go in. *With embarrassment*
Ha, ha . . . Your Lordship . . .

Both bow

LU CHYAN   That's enough, that's enough. This trip that you made: you've
really suffered.

DUNG CHAU
AND
SYWE BA   Oh, not that bad.

LU CHYAN   You're very tired!

SYWE BA   Not suffered, not tired.

LU CHYAN   Let me ask the two of you: where did you do the killing!

SYWE BA   Wild Boar Forest.

DUNG CHAU   Wild Boar Forest.

LU CHYAN   Wild Boar Forest. Oh! What a dangerous and treacherous place!
You wait until I report all to the minister, then I'll ask rewards
for the two of you.

SYWE BA   Many thanks, your Lordship. Many thanks, your Lordship.

LU CHYAN   Did you bring it back?

DUNG CHAU   Ah? *Thunderstruck*

LU CHYAN   The brand from Lin Chung's face.

DUNG CHAU   Brand? Ai ya, brand! Brand!

LU CHYAN Oh, oh! I can see by your looks that chances are you didn't kill him!

SYWE BA We lowered the sword all right – But just as we were going to kill him, he gave us a bit of trouble.

LU CHYAN Something went wrong again? Don't beat around the bush, talk!

DUNG CHAU Fellow, you tell him, you tell him!

SYWE BA Taking the prisoner, Lin Chung, on the way, we traveled to Wild Boar Forest; and just as we were about to kill dead Lin Chung, suddenly there came a big, fat monk! He rescued Lin Chung. Almost killed us.

LU CHYAN I gather from what you say: Lin Chung ran away?

DUNG CHAU Ran away? How could he dare to run away? There were the two of us guarding him, but that big, fat monk 'guarded' the two of us, step by step, right into Tsang Jou City.

LU CHYAN *spits*
Pei! You useless things! Not even able to carry out a little thing like this! You anger the Minister of War and still hope to live?

DUNG CHAU
AND
SYWE BA *in unison*
Nobleman Lu, how about putting in a good word for us!

LU CHYAN What's the name of that monk?

DUNG CHAU You don't know?

SYWE BA At Tsang Jou, I heard Lin Chung tell how the monk had pulled out by the roots the weeping willow tree at big Syan Gwo Temple.

LU CHYAN How's that? He was the one who pulled up the weeping willow at Syan Gwo Temple?

DUNG CHAU Ai, correct! He's the one who did it.

LU CHYAN *expressing that something has gone wrong*
Hai!

DUNG CHAU Yes, yes, yes!

LU CHYAN *dismisses the two guards*

SYWE BA We'll excuse ourselves now!

They exit

LU CHYAN *in anger*
Hmm, hmm. How daring of Lu Jr Shen! What a surprise he risked rescuing Lin Chung! Wait until I report this fully to the Minister, and let him know. A request to have an audience with the Minister Of War.

Enter GAU CHYOU

GAU CHYOU What's the matter?

LU CHYAN Just now Dung Chau, Sywe Ba came to report; those two fellows guarded the prisoner, Lin Chung. On the way to the Wild Boar Forest, Lin Chung was rescued by Lu Jr Shen. All went to Tsang Jou. I especially came to report this so you'd know.

GAU CHYOU How aggravating!

Sings

As I listen to these words,
My anger grows.
This daring and vicious monk has crossed me;
The more I think about the hate in my mind:
It's a case of pulling out the roots, to get rid of the weeds!

Calls

Come! Pass down an order to the Kaifeng officials to catch Lu Jr Shen. Make sure he's caught!

MILITARY
GUARD It shall be done.

Enter FU AN *and* GAU SHR DE

GAU CHYOU *to* FU AN

What happened? Why does Young Master look like this? Hurry, have someone take care of him. To a doctor! Go, go, right away!

Exit GUARD *and* GAU SHR DE

FU AN Your son took us along 'bride-snatching': we didn't plan it that way, but we failed in our bride snatching: Lin Chung's wife stabbed Young Master; you saw how Lin Chung's wife stabbed his Lordship?

GAU CHYOU This time she's gone too far, bring her here for sentencing.

FU AN She can't be brought here.

GAU CHYOU How's that?

FU AN After she stabbed young Master, then she cut her throat and died.

GAU CHYOU *In anger; expelling air*
Tu . . . What did I say to you before: Wait until the deputies had killed Lin Chung and had come back to report his death. *Then* go and propose marriage. You went on your own! Now that Young Master has been severely wounded, what punishment do you imagine you deserve!

FU AN Minister, don't be angry; think a moment. Young Master ordered us to go there; how could we have dared not go there. Minister, be generous with your favor.

GAU CHYOU If anything at all goes wrong with his Lordship, I must take your dog's life. Get out!

FU AN Yes, yes, yes.

Exits

GAU CHYOU   Hump! If I do not kill Lin Chung, then I swear I'm not a man. Lu Chyan!

LU CHYAN   Present.

GAU CHYOU   Where is Lin Chung now?

LU CHYAN   He must be in Tsang Jou.

GAU CHYOU   Take household guards with you; go to Tsang Jou, kill Lin Chung. Go quickly!

LU CHYAN   Your order will be carried out.

GAU CHYOU   *in anger*
Hey!

Exits

LU CHYAN   Household guards come present yourselves.

HOUSEHOLD
GUARDS   What are your orders?

LU CHYAN   The Minister has passed down the order, telling us to go without stop to Tsang Jou. There's a big reward for killing Lin Chung. Let's go to Tsang Jou now.

HOUSEHOLD
GUARDS   Ah!

All exit

SCENE 13   *Before the entrance to Shan Shen Temple. Enter an old soldier who has given refuge to* LIN CHUNG

LAU JYUN   Ah! This snow storm has been fierce. Without warning the weight of the snow crushed the tent. Fortunately, I was in the field, picking up firewood. Otherwise the snow would have killed me inside the tent. How unfortunate that tonight Drillmaster Lin and I don't have a place to stay. Ai ya, for now I'll go to Shan Shen Temple and escape for a little bit the windy cold. I'll wait for Drillmaster Lin to come back. Then we'll talk about what to do. Ai! *Exits*

LIN CHUNG *enters, carrying a spear and a gourd filled with wine*

LIN CHUNG   Unh Hunh! *Clears his throat* Ya!

Sings

Snow flakes fly;
A north wind blows;
It cuts to the bones,
Making one cold.
The past is like a dream,
Like a dream is my escape from the edge of death!

Recites

The heavy drifting snow drives against the face.
Gusts of north wind cut to the bone –
It's very cold.

I, Lin Chung, caught by a villain, drift and waste in Tsang Jou. But now I've the great honor to be taken care of by a woodsman, who recommended me to the military prisoner's ward; there to settle down as a foot soldier and guard the horse-fodder. Once arrived in Tsang Jou, I was separated from Benevolent Brother Lu, who returned to the Eastern Capital – to this day I do not know what has happened to my wife.

Enter LU JR SHEN, *quietly, bearing his staff*

LU JR SHEN   *slapping* LIN CHUNG *on the back*
Ah, Virtuous Brother, 'Clumsy Brother' is here.

LIN CHUNG   *surprised and happy*
Benevolent Brother, you've come back!

LU JR SHEN   I've returned.

They embrace

LIN CHUNG   Ai, ya, Benevolent Brother, ah – you – I've missed you a great deal.

LU JR SHEN   Your Brother also missed you. Virtuous Brother, after I left Tsang Jou did anyone take advantage of you?

LIN CHUNG   I had the very great honor of being taken care of by a woodsman. Absolutely nobody molested me. Benevolent Brother, you and I, Brothers, have not been separated for long; and again you've come to Tsang Jou! Do you mean to tell me that you didn't reach the Eastern Capital?

LU JR SHEN   Don't speak of it anymore! That thief Gau Chyou learned that 'Clumsy Brother' rescued you in the Wild Board Forest. As soon as I arrived in the Eastern Capital, he sent people in all directions to catch me. Hearing about this, I got angry and burned down the vegetable garden. Then traveling by night I came back to Tsang Jou to search for Virtuous Brother. Let's you and I rush out at once to Mt. Lyang.*

LIN CHUNG   *startled, and gestures to stop* LU JR SHEN's *speaking*
Don't make a sound!

They look at each other, pause

Benevolent Brother, go on talking.

LU JR SHEN   Let's rush at once to Mt. Lyang to gather together righteous men and make them into soldiers. We *must* kill Gau Chyou, that villainous theif, and so avenge you and relieve my hatred.

LIN CHUNG   *hesitantly*
The woodsman had also spoken of this. Ah, Benevolent Brother, when you had arrived in the Eastern Capital this time, do you happen to know how my family was?

* This is the most important mountain of the Wild Boar Forest. It can be compared in its fame to Sherwood Forest.

LU JR SHEN Your Lady . . .

LIN CHUNG What happened?

LU JR SHEN Was forced by Gau Chyou's doglike son, in ten thousand different ways, to yield . . . she . . . slashed her throat and died.
LIN CHUNG *reacts with shock*. Virtuous Brother, from this day
forth, you have nothing more to think about but . . . LU JR
SHEN *advances excitely*; LIN CHUNG *backs away*

LIN CHUNG *halfheartedly mumbling agreement*
Ung!

As LU *advances*, LIN CHUNG *backs away a step* *

LU JR SHEN *advances*
Gather righteous men and make them soldiers.

LIN CHUNG *retreats*
Ung!

LU JR SHEN *advances*
Wipe out that peerless villain . . .

LIN CHUNG *retreats*
Ung!

LU JR SHEN *advances*
. . . thus to avenge you and to relieve my hatred!

LIN CHUNG *advances*
Fine! Now I say to my Benevolent Brother, – Yes! Quickly give
the word to the woodsman.

LU JR SHEN *withdraws a step*
Yes!

* This elaborate pattern of advancing and retreating shows first that Lin
is dispirited and then that he decides to forget about the past and move
to a new life.

LIN CHUNG *advances*
Then we'll rush at once to Mt. Lyang.

LU JR SHEN *retreats a step*
Yes!

LIN CHUNG *advances*
Having given the word, come back immediately!

LU JR SHEN *retreats*
Yes!

LIN CHUNG *advances*
Little Brother will be waiting at the tent.

LU JR SHEN *withdraws*
Yes!

LIN CHUNG *advances*
You . . . take care!

LU JR SHEN Ya, ya, ya! I'll go, then come back.

LIN CHUNG Please!

> LU JR SHEN *exits. His feelings are mixed with sorrow and grati-tude; tears come to his eyes*

Hai! The way things have come to pass, I, Lin Chung have no other cares now! Let me return to the tent and wait for Benevolent Brother Lu; together we'll make big plans.

Recites

Even though the hero has no worries,
Still has he tears.
But when a deep hatred has not been wiped out,
A hero holds back his tears!

Sings

Bereft of cares,
I resolve to take myself to Mt. Lyang.

LAU JYUN *offstage sings*
The sunset breezes stir the sands;
Red clouds darken,
A lonely wild duck finds it difficult
To perch against the wind, the snow, the cold!

LIN CHUNG *continues the singing*
I hear a voice within the Temple.

LAU JYUN *enters*
Ah, Brother Lin, you've come back?

LIN CHUNG Elder Brother, while snow fills the air and winds cut to the bone, why are you not in the tent, avoiding the cold? Did you come here by yourself?

LAU JYUN Hai! After you left, Brother Lin, a fierce snowstorm downed the tent; It was my good fortune to be in the field gathering wood. Otherwise I would have been crushed to death, inside the tent. So I came here just to get out of the cold.

LIN CHUNG Since the tent has been crushed by the snow, you and I will stay in the temple tonight. I have brought wine; we'll drink deeply and escape the cold.

LAU JYUN Fine, Brother Lin. First, you enter the temple, wait while I go into the field – I'll pick up twigs so that we may keep warm.

LIN CHUNG *his thoughts wander*
I put you to much trouble –
One draws the sword to cut water,
But water still flows.

LAU JYUN One lifts the cup to drown sorrow,
But the sorrow grows with sorrow.

LAU JYUN *circles the stage, preparing to exit*

LIN CHUNG Snow fills heaven and earth,
But how difficult to let fall one's hatred!

LAU JYUN Ai! Green Mountains without number grow bald! *

LAU JYUN *exits, and* LIN CHUNG *enters the temple. Enter* LU CHYAN *and eight* HOUSEHOLD GUARDS

LU CHYAN Brothers, as I look ahead of me, I see we've already arrived at the military feeding ground; Lin Chung is surely inside, loafing and sleeping. We are going to circle and encircle him; set out fire and burn the fields! By no means, let anyone escape. Brothers, set the fire!

HOUSEHOLD
GUARDS *Mime setting the fire*
Yes, set the fire, set the fire!

LU CHYAN *Laughs aloud with contempt*
Ha, ha! I see a big fire rush into the skies, it's just like the "Red Wall" † – I call out Lin Chung: Lin Chung, you are to die, bound for Yellow Springs.‡ Blame me not for having evil intentions and a black heart!

Turns to the HOUSEHOLD GUARDS

I say, Brothers, wait for the fire to go out; then we'll pick up a few pieces of Lin Chung's bones, bring them back, so we have proof for getting the reward. *He shudders from the cold* The snow is getting worse. Brothers, stand by. I'll go and rest a bit in the temple. By all means don't go far. *Gloating, he walks toward the temple, opens the gate, and with shock sees* LIN CHUNG

You – are Lin Chung?

* An expression that means 'Age ultimately comes to all.'
† In the famous Chinese novel *Three Kingdoms*, a great battle was fought here.
‡ Yellow Springs is the land of the dead.

LIN CHUNG   I am the Lin Chung you cannot harm!

LU CHYAN   Lin Chung, without permission you left the field. Now it is on fire. What punishment do you deserve?

LIN CHUNG   Hm, so, thief, today you traced me here – and still you hope to live!

LU CHYAN   You, you – with death so very near to you, you still dare to be so bold! *With a wink,* LU CHYAN *signals to his guards; they surround* LIN CHUNG

LIN CHUNG   *fearlessly surveys the guards*
I ready myself to test the skill of your sword!

LIN CHUNG *advances toward* LU CHYAN, *who withdraws*

LU CHYAN   *laughs cunningly*
Ha, ha! I fear that by my sword you're going to become a ghost!

LIN CHUNG   Thief Lu! I cannot wait to eat your flesh. Only then will the hatred within me be at peace.

LU CHYAN   On guard.

HOUSEHOLD
GUARDS   Kill! Kill! Kill!

Sword play and acrobatics. LIN CHUNG *kills all the guards, and subdues* LU CHYAN

LU CHYAN   *cornered*
Virtuous Brother, Lin Chung!

LIN CHUNG   *Recites*
I, Lin Chung,
What had you against me?
To kill may be forgiven;
But to blunder never!
Here in front of the Shan Shen Temple
I take your life.

LU CHYAN   Virtuous Brother, all things may be talked out between us. Don't break the bond between the two brothers!

LIN CHUNG   I kill the person who has wronged me!

LU CHYAN   Ah, Virtuous Brother!

Enter hurriedly LU JR SHEN *with his staff.* LIN CHUNG *raises his sword, killing* LU CHYAN

LU JR SHEN   Virtuous Brother . . .

From the fighting, LIN CHUNG *acts confused. He fails to recognize* LU JR SHEN. *He turns and points his sword at him.* LU *parries the blow from the sword with his staff*

What has happened?

LU CHUNG *points to the body of* LU CHYAN. LU JR SHEN *grasps the situation and strikes the body with his staff.* LIN CHUNG *hacks at the body with his sword*

LU JR SHEN
AND
LIN CHUNG   Ha, ha, ha!

Curtain

Taking Tiger Mountain by Strategy

COLLECTIVELY WRITTEN AND
REVISED BY MEMBERS OF THE
PEKING OPERA TROUPE
IN SHANGHAI
TRANSLATED
BY RICHARD E. STRASSBERG

CHARACTERS

YANG DZ RUNG scout platoon leader in the Chinese People's Liberation Army (PLA)

SHAU JYAN PWO regimental chief of staff in the PLA

LI YUNG CHI railroad worker

CHANG BAU a hunter's daughter

SHEN DE HWA deputy leader of a scout platoon in the PLA

MEDICAL ORDERLY nurse in the PLA

LITTLE GWO guard in the PLA

JUNG JR CHENG
LYU HUNG YE } soldiers in the PLA
LWO CHANG JYANG

OTHER SOLDIERS

HUNTER CHANG father of CHANG BAU

MOTHER LI mother of LI YUNG CHI

JANG DA SHAN railroad worker

LI YUNG CHI'S WIFE

PEOPLE REPRESENTING
THE MASSES

MOUNTAIN VULTURE head of the bandits on Tiger Mountain, leader of the Kuomintang 'Fifth Peace Preservation Brigade in the Eastern Heilungjyang region' *

* The Kuomintang is the Nationalist Party under Chiang Kai-shek. Heilungjyang (Heilungkiang) is in Northern Manchuria.

LWAN PING liason adjutant under Horse Cudgel Syu, head of
the bandits on Nipple Mountain

BANDIT CHIEF OF STAFF

BANDIT CHIEF ADJUTANT

BANDIT CAPTAIN

GROUP OF EIGHT
INVINCIBLES

OTHER BANDITS

SCENE 1 Unfurling Victory: The Army Advances

The Winter of 1946, somewhere in Northeast China. A deep, mountainous forest, lying under a heavy snow. A pursuit detachment of the PLA, *the Red Flag at the lead, enters quickly. The army, in full battle array, marches along a mountain trail. The soldiers perform a dance as they confront the wind and plow through the snow*

LWO CHANG

JYANG Halt the Advance!

The soldiers form ranks

Reporting to the Chief of Staff! We've reached a fork in the road.

SHAU

JYAN PWO Then we'll rest here a while.

LWO Yes sir! Lyu Hung Ye!

LYU

HUNG YE Here!

LWO Stand guard!

LYU Yes sir! *Exit*

LWO We'll rest here!

SOLDIERS Yes sir!

LITTLE GWO *hands* SHAU *a map.* SHAU *looks it over and then observes the terrain*

LWO Supply Chief! We'll rest here.

Voices in the background echo 'Rest here!' The sound of horses neighing. The soldiers stamp their feet to keep warm and brush off the snow

SHAU   Is everyone tired?

SOLDIERS   No, we're not!

SHAU   Good! Comrades Yang Dz Rung and Shen De Hwa have gone
up ahead to reconnoiter. This is the place where we're supposed
to meet again. The Regiment Party Committee organized this
pursuit detachment in accordance with Chairman Mao's instructions 'Establish firm bases in the Northeast.' We must arouse the
masses in the Peony River area, extinguish the local bandits, consolidate the rear, coordinate the troops in the field and pulverize
the U.S.-Chiang Kai-shek offensive – these are all tasks of great
strategic importance. That old bandit, Mountain Vulture, has
escaped deep into the mountains. We've been marching in the
wind and snow for a good many days now and still haven't found
him. Let's raise high our spirit of continuous fighting. *Forcefully*

'Be resolute
With no fear of sacrifice
Eliminate all difficulties'

SHAU AND
SOLDIERS   'To go and obtain Victory!'

Enter LYU HUNG YE

LYU   Reporting! Yang and the others have returned from scouting.

Enter YANG DZ RUNG, SHEN DE HWA. *They salute*

YANG
DZ RUNG   Reporting back!

SHAU   Comrade Dz Rung, you've had a rough time.

YANG   We went scouting in disguise as ordered, and along the way we
saved a mute child in an isolated ravine. Following the directions
that his father gave us, we were able to get to Black Dragon
Valley. We searched about there and investigated the movements
of Mountain Vulture:

SHAU Good!

YANG *sings*
　　　　Bandits come and go by here,
　　　　blatantly like a parade.
　　　　Calling themselves 'The Third Regiment
　　　　of the Fifth Peace Preservation Brigade.'
　　　　Last night Black Dragon Valley saw another raid.

　　　　Mountain Vulture, wolfish and cruel, has
　　　　crimes that overflow heaven.
　　　　After looting, his gang crawled back to
　　　　their lair in Jya Pi Valley
　　　　But now I figure these bandits are holed up on Tiger Mountain.

SHAU Comrades! We've caught on to the Vulture's trail.
　　　　Now we must carefully track him down. Lwo Chang Jyang!

LWO Here!

SHAU Tonight we'll make camp in Black Dragon Valley!

LWO Yes sir!

SHAU Comrade Dz Rung!

YANG Here!

SHAU We still want to learn some more about the enemy's situation.
　　　　Take Shen De Hwa –

SHEN Here!

SHAU Jung Jr Cheng –

JUNG Here!

SHAU And Lyu Hung Ye –

LYU Here!

SHAU   And continue on scouting in front.

YANG   Yes sir!

SHAU   Leave now.

They freeze in a martial pose, then exit

SCENE 2   The Looting of Jya Pi Valley

> *Dusk. Just outside the village of Jya Pi Valley. Withered trees lie strewn about. Along the sides of the valley are deep crags. The Kuomintang 'Fifth Peace Preservation Brigade,' which is Mountain Vulture's bandit group, is returning to the mountains. The road goes through Jya Pi Valley.* MOUNTAIN VULTURE *takes a look at the village*

BANDIT
CHIEF
ADJUTANT   Third Brother, we've made off with quite a bit along the way this time. Jya Pi Valley is right on our doorstep – we'd better not plunder them.

BANDIT
CHIEF OF
STAFF   Right. 'A rabbit won't nibble the grass near his hole,' as they say.

MOUNTAIN
VULTURE   Forget about that! Go and grab me some of those paupers and bring them back to do repair work. I want both men and women.

CHIEF OF
STAFF   I understand.

> *The* CHIEF OF STAFF *leads a group of bandits into the village. The* CHIEF ADJUTANT *is about to go along when* MOUNTAIN VULTURE *calls him*

VULTURE Adjutant! Its been about ten days since Howling Wolf went to find Lwan Ping.

ADJUTANT Uh huh, I've been pretty concerned about it myself.

VULTURE When we get back to Tiger Mountain, the first thing we have to do is increase our forces.

ADJUTANT Right. If Howling Wolf can find Lwan Ping and get hold of the Agent's Map, the whole Peony River area will belong to us.

VULTURE Commissioner Hou has been looking all over for this map, though – we've got to keep him from getting it.

ADJUTANT Third Brother, don't worry. Howling Wolf and Lwan Ping are sworn brothers. The map won't fly away from them.

VULTURE On the surface, the Americans are arranging peace negotiations between the Communists and Nationalists but at the same time, they're helping Chiang Kai-shek transport his forces.* I heard that old Chiang himself is in Shenyang to personally supervise the fighting. In three months he'll eliminate the Communist army on both sides of the Great Wall. I think our time has come!

ADJUTANT Good! When the Nationalist armies arrive, you will be commander of Northern Manchuria! Jang Dzwo Lin, Manchugwo, Chiang Kai-shek † – none of them could have done without you!

VULTURE Ha! Ha! Ha!

From the village, a dog's cry is heard. MOUNTAIN VULTURE *and the* ADJUTANT *enter the village. Fire erupts from all corners. People screaming. Enter* LI YUNG CHI, *running onstage with a hunter's knife holding his kill*

---

* This refers to the negotiations held in Chungking under General George Marshall.
† Jang Dzwo Lin (Chang Tso-lin) was warlord of Manchuria until killed by the Japanese in 1928. Manchugwo (Manchukuo) was the name of the puppet Japanese state established in Manchuria in 1932. Chiang Kai-shek regained control of the area at the end of World War II.

LI YUNG CHI *Sings*
Fiery light engulfs the sky,
People shout.
Mothers scream for their children,
who call to them in the uproar.
The bandits have returned to plunder,
burning and killing once more.
It would be well worth my life
to try and settle the score.

*Bandits forcibly grab a group of young men and women villagers
and proceed to bind them together with rope.* LI YUNG CHI *continues fighting the bandits. When the group is firmly tied up,
they are beaten and forced to exit.* LI YUNG CHI'S WIFE *is pulled
onstage, her mother-in-law hurriedly following, holding her
baby. A bandit captain takes the baby, runs to the edge of the
valley and cruelly hurls the child into the gully.* LI YUNG CHI
*enters in a fury and desperately attacks the bandits. His left arm
is injured. Enter* MOUNTAIN VULTURE, *who shoots at* LI

WIFE Yung Chi!

LI'S WIFE *thrusts herself in front of* LI *to shield him. She is shot
and killed. Exit* MOUNTAIN VULTURE *and bandits. Grief stricken,*
LI *gazes at his* WIFE

LI My wife . . . my wife . . .

MOTHER LI *rushing over, in great sorrow*
Daughter!

LI *Sings*
Disaster strikes like a clap of thunder
My breast is inflamed with fiery anger
I swear I will avenge –

Mountain Vulture!
I'll hack you to pieces for this
blood debt – you murderer!

LI *hurls himself at the bandits. They overpower him and tie him
up. He continues to struggle with all his might*

MOTHER LI Yung Chi . . .

LI Mother . . .

LI *is carried off*

LI Mother! Mother! Mother!

MOTHER LI *crawling after him*
Yung Chi!

SCENE 3 Bitterness in the Mountains

Afternoon. An isolated mountain valley. Inside a small wooden hut, a table with bowls and chopsticks spread about. CHANG BAU *is in the hut cleaning up the table.* HUNTER CHANG *is gazing outside*

CHANG BAU Father, that man and woman who just came were really impossible – they ate up all the meat that we'd just caught.

HUNTER CHANG Chang Bau, do you know who that man and woman were?

CHANG BAU Didn't the man say he was from the Chinese People's Liberation Army?

HUNTER CHANG Hah! Eight years ago, when I was dragged up to Tiger Mountain, I saw him there. He's a bandit called Howling Wolf.

CHANG BAU Ah!

HUNTER CHANG We can't stay here any more! Let's pack our things quickly and go to your Uncle Da Shan in Jya Pi Valley.

CHANG BAU   Yes. *She gets her things together*

HUNTER
CHANG   *to himself*
Those two fur traders who came by a few days ago said that the
Communist came to their village and helped the poor to create
a new life. I wonder if it's true or not?

CHANG BAU   Father, those two fur traders were certainly good people. If they
hadn't saved me from the snow, I would have quickly frozen to
death!

HUNTER
CHANG   Yes. Now – quickly!

HUNTER CHANG *ties a bundle.* CHANG BAU *takes some skins off the
wall and notices people's shadows through the window*

CHANG BAU   Father! Someone's coming again!

HUNTER CHANG *quickly puts his hand over* CHANG BAU's *mouth*

HUNTER
CHANG   Keep quiet!

The two listen intensely. YANG DZ RUNG, SHEN DE HWA, JUNG JR
CHENG *and* LYU HUNG YE *enter wearing white capes and hoods
which hide the Red Star insignia on their caps. They jump
through the snow and make their way over to the hut*

YANG   *sings*
Closely we followed a suspicious fellow
only to lose his trail in the snow.

SHEN   Say, Old Yang – isn't this the Hunter Chang's house?

YANG   You're right, it is. *Continues to sing*
We'll drop by the hunter's place again
and see if he can solve our problem.

Comrades Shen and Lyu!

SHEN AND
LYU   Yes sir! *Exit*

YANG   Little Jung! Stand guard!

JUNG   Yes sir! *Exits*

YANG   *Goes over to the hut and knocks on the door*
Say there, old friend!

    HUNTER CHANG *nervously comes out of the hut*

HUNTER
CHANG   *looking over the stranger in front of him*
You're . . .

YANG   Don't you recognize me? I'm the fur trader who came by the other day.

HUNTER
CHANG   Fur trader?

YANG   Yes.

    CHANG BAU *has been listening and runs out*

YANG   *to* CHANG BAU
Little Brother, your father doesn't recognize me. Didn't I bring you back home that day?

    Looking him over carefully, CHANG BAU *is about to speak when she stops and just nods*

YANG   *observing all this but not letting on that he understands, his expression is unchanged*
You're a bright child!

HUNTER
CHANG   *carefully looks at* YANG *and recognizes him*
Oh! You're Yang the trader!

YANG Right!

HUNTER
CHANG Sure! And we discovered we were neighbors from back home. Please come in, sit down!

All enter the hut

YANG *to* CHANG BAU
Are you feeling better now?

HUNTER
CHANG *cutting him off*
He's a mute.

YANG Oh? Why . . . yes.

HUNTER
CHANG You're in business and yet also serve as a soldier – really, what do you do?

YANG I'm really not a merchant at all. *He pulls off his hood and reveals the Red Star* I'm a member of the Chinese People's Liberation Army!

HUNTER
CHANG *half-suspiciously*
You're also in the People's Liberation Army?

YANG That's right. Have you ever seen anyone from the PLA before?

HUNTER
CHANG *cautiously*
No . . . I haven't.

YANG *sitting down on a bench*
Last time we came, I didn't tell you much. We've come over from Shandung Province – troops led by Chairman Mao and the Communist Party.

HUNTER
CHANG Ah? That's really far away. What are you doing here?

YANG Fighting off bandits. *He picks up an axe and slams it into a block of wood*

HUNTER
CHANG Fighting the bandits? Can you do it?

YANG *jumps up*
Our batallions are not far behind us. The Chinese People's Liberation Army has fought a good many victories in the Northeast. The entire Peony River area has been liberated. We've obliterated most of the bandits already. The only ones left are Mountain Vulture and his obstinate gang who have fled into the mountains. We'll certainly eliminate them with all speed!

HUNTER
CHANG *bitterly*
Ah, Vulture . . .

YANG Old Chang, Mountain Vulture has been despoiling this area long enough! A father and son like you two – seeking shelter in this deep forest – you must have suffered great wrongs.

HUNTER CHANG *sits down and violently grasps hold of the axe*

YANG Old Chang – speak out!

HUNTER
CHANG *unwilling to bring up a painful past*
It's been eight years . . . but let's not talk about it. *He throws the axe down*

CHANG BAU *uncontrollably*
Father – !

HUNTER
CHANG *startled at first, then bitter*
Chang Bau, you . . .

YANG *with deep emotion*
Child! The Communist Party and Chairman Mao will back you
up. Go on and speak!

CHANG BAU Father, I'll talk! I'll talk!

Sings

Eight years ago,
In wind and snow,
Heaven dealt us a grievous blow.

My grandmother killed,
My mother a prisoner,
It was Mountain Vulture who sealed their fate.
Uncle Da Shan took me in
But fleeing, mother lost her life
Only father made good his escape.
We retreated deep into these hills
Where he feared those devils
Would look on me as bait.
So I agreed to
Pose as a mute
And dress like a boy,
Something I can hardly tolerate.

Father and daughter hunt food in the cliffs
As long as the sun continues to shine
At nightfall grandmother enters father's thoughts
While mother is never away from mine.

I often gaze at the stars and look at the moon
Hoping to see the sun rise over the deep mountains
Hoping to be able to tell all this to someone,
Hoping to one day wear girls' clothes again
Hoping to wipe clean this eight-year debt of blood!

How I hate that I can't sprout wings!
I'd grab a hunting knife
Fly to the mountain top
And kill all those wolves before I could stop!

Father!

She throws herself into HUNTER CHANG's *arms*

YANG   *excitedly sings*
Little Chang Bau accuses the bandits of their crimes.
Each word in blood
Each word in tears
All under heaven who are people oppressed have a debt of blood
          and tears.
We want revenge and justice
Revenge and justice.
Debts of blood are washed away in blood!

Exterminate Mountain Vulture
And the people will achieve liberation.
Become the masters of your own lives
And you'll see the sun shine in these deep mountains.
From now on follow the saving star of the Communist Party.
The land itself will change its cast.
This place is just like our old home.
Beautiful days forever lie just ahead!

HUNTER
CHANG   *greatly moved*
Old Yang!

Both sit down. CHANG BAU *devotedly hands* YANG DZ RUNG *a glass of water.* YANG *empties the glass*

HUNTER
CHANG   Old Yang, these words have touched deep into my heart. Ah, but fighting Mountain Vulture isn't easy. He controls nine groups, twenty-seven forts. He can attack here, defend there and then slip away. There's no one who can catch him.

YANG   Yes. I understand it's hard to rush in on him using the mountain roads.

HUNTER
CHANG   True. There's only one clear path in front – high and steep. In addition there are closely knit defenses. Who could make it up there?

YANG   How did you come down from there that year?

HUNTER
CHANG   In the back there's a dangerous road full of sloping crags and overhanging cliffs. No one dares go there and the bandits never bothered to defend it. Eight years ago I came down from there. If I hadn't fallen onto a tree, I would have broken every bone in my body.

YANG   Old Chang, the situation you've brought up is very useful. If we all unite with one heart, there's no mountain peak we can't scale.

HUNTER
CHANG   Right! I've longed for this day. Ha! Ha! Ha! Old Yang, I don't consider you a stranger anymore. Just now a man and woman came by. The man was clearly a bandit but he said he was from the PLA.

CHANG BAU   My father saw him on Tiger Mountain. He's called Howling Wolf.

YANG   Howling Wolf! What did he say?

HUNTER
CHANG   He called the woman his sister-in-law. What else did he say? Uh . . . he said he was a sworn brother of Lwan Ping.

YANG   *blurts out*
Lwan Ping? *Jumps up*

HUNTER
CHANG   *also jumps up*
From what I could see, the woman was Lwan Ping's wife. Howling Wolf was arguing with her for some time – over getting hold of some map.

CHANG BAU The Agent's Map!

HUNTER
CHANG That's right.

YANG The Agent's Map?

JUNG JR CHENG *enters and goes into the hut*

JUNG Sir, Old Shen and the others have returned.

SHEN DE HWA, LYU HUNG YE *enter and go into the hut*

SHEN Old Yang – we've found a woman's corpse northeast of here. Next to her there was a glove with blood on it. *He hands the glove to* YANG DZ RUNG

LYU The wind and snow were too much and covered all the footprints. I don't know where the murderer escaped to.

YANG Old Chang, have you ever seen this glove before?

HUNTER
CHANG *looks at the glove*
Uh huh . . . this belongs to Howling Wolf.

YANG *decisively*
He's certainly the one who killed her and stole the Agent's Map. Comrades, this case is very complex and involves the Lwan Ping we're searching for. Lyu Hung Ye!

LYU Here!

YANG We'll have to somehow provoke the assailant. You go back and report the situation to the Chief of Staff. I suggest we investigate Lwan Ping and get hold of the Agent's Map.

LYU Yes sir! *Runs off*

YANG Old Chang, things are very pressing. I can't stay and talk with you any more. Here's some food I'm leaving you.

YANG DZ RUNG *opens a bag and gives some provisions to* HUNTER CHANG. SHEN DE HWA *also takes some food from his bag and gives it to* CHANG BAU.

HUNTER
CHANG   Old Yang!

SHEN   Please, keep it!

CHANG BAU   *greatly moved*
Dad . . .

YANG   So long! *Turns and is about to leave*

HUNTER
CHANG   Old Yang, where are you going?

YANG   To capture Howling Wolf!

HUNTER
CHANG   No, you can't! Howling Wolf has certainly run off to Tiger Mountain. The roads here are hard to travel anyway. With this blizzard sealing off the mountains, a stranger won't be able to find anything. Come one! My child and I will show you the way!

YANG   *to* HUNTER CHANG, *excitedly*
Old Chang . . . thanks!

HUNTER
CHANG   Let's go!

All freeze in a dramatic pose.

SCENE 4   Devising a Plan

Early morning in Black Dragon Valley. The pursuit detachment has spent the night. Brightly burning coals provide warmth inside the command post. Outside, a fierce wind howls as the snow whirls. Majestic mountains and a heavy forest in the background

SHAU *self-composed, sings*
> A frigid wind blows down through the trees,
> Its surging howls shake Jya Pi Valley.

A gust of wind blows the door open. SHAU JYAN PWO *goes over to the door and looks out in the distance* SHAU *sings*

> Watching the snow dance up in the sky,
> Against majestic mountains clad in silver finery.
> What a fine piece of northern scenery!

Closes the door, then sings

> Our mountains and rivers,
> Graceful yet firm,
> With myriad forms of life abound.
> How can we ever feel safe and sound,
> While tigers and wolves roam around?

> The Party Central Committee leads the way.
> Flames of Revolution can't be ignored.
> The PLA is on the march.
> Carrying the hopes of the People forward.
> The Red Flag will fly throughout our land.
> Why fear the U.S.-Chiang gang-up?
> Though they preach negotiation,
> They strike from behind.
> Shoot in broad daylight,
> Snipe in the dark,
> And have a hundred tricks in hand.
> How can they stop those who,
> Grasping justice,
> Carry hatred in their breasts?
> One against ten,
> We'll still wipe out their whole reactionary band!

Enter YANG DZ RUNG

YANG Reporting, Sir!

SHAU *recognizing the voice*
      Old Yang!

      YANG *enters the house.* SHAU *goes forward to meet him*

SHAU Did you catch the murderer yet?

YANG We've got him! Here's a letter and an Agent's Map which we found on him. *Hands over the letter and map*

SHAU Good!

YANG The paths around here are hard to find but Hunter Chang acted as our guide. The murderer was posing as one of our scouts but Hunter Chang exposed him. He then admitted he was from Tiger Mountain. His name is Li Chung Hau, nicknamed Howling Wolf.

SHAU Great! The Hunter has been a great help to us. Chairman Mao taught us: 'The revolutionary war is a war of the masses. Only if we mobilize the masses can we wage war. Only if we rely on the masses can we wage war.' If we were to draw away from the masses, we couldn't even move half a step!

YANG Right! Hunter Chang volunteered information on two ways up the mountain. Based on his description, I drew a rough map.

      Hands over the sketch

      Howling Wolf agreed that this path in front of the mountain is quite clear and unfortified. He says it's easy to climb.

SHAU Hah! He's obviously lying. Have you made arrangements for the Hunter and his daughter?

YANG We left some food with the Hunter. They plan to move to Jya Pi Valley.

SHAU Good. *Looks at the letter and the Agent's Map*
      Uh, Old Yang, Lwan Ping never confessed anything about this map.

YANG   That's right. Howling Wolf said that the Agent's Map shows over three hundred secret contact points of the Nipple Mountain gang in the Northeast. This is a big problem!

SHAU   Lwan Ping's already been caught. Let's question him immediately and get this Agent's Map thing cleared up.

YANG   Good, I'll go fetch Lwan Ping. *About to leave*

SHAU   Uh, Old Yang, Lwan Ping is an old adversary of yours. Why not question him yourself?

YANG   Yes sir!

SHAU *goes into the back room*

YANG   *to the soldier on guard outside*
        Little Chang!

LITTLE
CHANG   Here!

YANG   Bring Lwan Ping!

LITTLE
CHANG   Yes sir!

LITTLE GWO *brings* LWAN PING *onstage. Both enter the house.* LWAN PING *sees* YANG DZ RUNG *and is about to go forward and salute.* YANG *motions him to a seat*

YANG   Lwan Ping!

LWAN PING   Yes!

YANG   How is your confession coming along?

LWAN   I want to make a clean sweep. I'll tell whatever there is to tell.

YANG   There's still some information you haven't given over yet.

LWAN Officer, except for the clothes on my back, I don't possess a thing.

YANG *suddenly*
What about a map?

LWAN PING A map?

YANG An Agent's Map!

LWAN *startled*
Uh? *Composes himself* Let me think . . . *Pretends to be deep in thought* Uh, why yes, yes, its come to me. I heard that Horse Cudgel Syu has a secret Agent's Map.

YANG You just *heard?*

LWAN Officer, make no mistake. Horse Cudgel Syu considered this map extremely valuable. I've never seen it myself.

YANG Lwan Ping, you ought to understand our policy!

LWAN I understand. Lenience to those who confess, severity to those who resist.

YANG Now, I ask you: What did you do on Nipple Mountain?

LWAN You know that. I was a liason adjutant.

YANG A liason adjutant who doesn't know anything about contact points and who never saw an Agent's Map? Hah! It looks like you don't want to tell the truth!

LWAN PING *tries to appear helpless*

YANG Take him away!

LITTLE GWO Let's go!

LWAN *holding on to the chair, terror-stricken*
No, No! I . . . *Slaps his own face* I ought to die, I ought to die for trying to deceive you, Officer! I'll tell the truth now – there is an Agent's Map. It shows secret contact spots for Horse Cudgel Syu all over the Northeast – more than three hundred of them! It's in my wife's hands now. If you were to release me, I could get it back from her and present it to you, Officer. That way I could earn lenient treatment by making some contribution. *Bows*

YANG Besides those three hundred spots, where else did you have contacts?

LWAN Where else? Only Mountain Vulture. But Mountain Vulture has long wanted to become ruler of Northern Manchuria. He and Horse Cudgel Syu get along on the surface but not really. I've had very little contact with him. Last year, on Mountain Vulture's birthday, I was invited to his Hundred Chickens Feast but I didn't go.

YANG *listening intently*
You'd better come clean and confess everything! Write out the whole situation about the contact spots in detail!

LWAN Yes sir! Yes sir!

YANG Take him out!

LITTLE GWO Let's go! *Conducts Lwan Ping offstage*

SHAU JYAN PWO *comes out of the back room*

YANG That fellow's a sneaky one!

SHAU *jokingly*
The sneakiest fox can't escape a good hunter! What he's told us about the Agent's Map tallies with Howling Wolf's story.

YANG He unwittingly let slip something about the Hundred Chickens Feast.

SHAU Yes.

YANG This letter shows that Mountain Vulture has again invited him to the feast on the mountain. But I still feel there's something wrong here.

SHAU Right.

Enter SHEN DE HWA

SHEN Reporting, sir!

SHAU Come in!

SHEN DE HWA *enters the house*

SHEN Chief of Staff, the comrades are anxious to attack Tiger Mountain. They've written a request for battle assignments.

SHAU You're the head of all this, I suppose.

SHEN Well, sir, I . . .

SHAU Ha! Ha! Ha! Ha!

Sits down by the fire

I can well understand how the comrades feel. Our brothers in the other units have already closed off all the important roads and ferry points in the Peony River area – Mountain Vulture can't get away now! But that bastard is hard to deal with. Haven't we all discussed it several times? If we were to attack in full force, it would be like trying to hit a fly with your fist – that won't do. We could lure them down the mountain one by one and pick them off but we're pressed for time. This requires a special kind of warfare. We ought to remember Chairman Mao's instructions: despise the enemy strategically but take him seriously when it comes to tactics! Comrade De Hwa, go and call another Democratic Meeting. Based on this new situation, go and discuss things once more.

SHEN   Yes sir! *Exits*

       YANG DZ RUNG *is about to exit*

SHAU   Uh, Old Yang, what do you think?

YANG   I think we should question Howling Wolf again and get a clearer
       picture of the Hundred Chickens Feast on Tiger Mountain.

SHAU   Very good. I'll wait for your recommendations.

YANG   Yes sir! *Exits*

SHAU   *sings*
       We've studied the enemy's position now.
       In the past few days we've learned quite a bit.
       Battle plans debated back and forth,
       Finally we found one that will fit.
       Tiger Mountain is a stronghold based on
       Fortresses and tunnels tightly knit.
       It seems best to depend on strategy
       And achieve our victory by wit.

       We'll choose an able man to pose as one of their own,
       And pierce his way into the enemy's lair.
       Then we can strike from within and without,
       Wiping out the bandits before they're aware.
       This duty weighs down like a thousand pound load.
       Who would be best for us to send there?

       Thinks, then sings

       Yang Dz Rung has the requirements to pick up this load,
       Hailing from a solid hired-peasant family.
       Since childhood he's struggled along the life-death road.
       Full of hatred, he longs for a saving star to see.
       Now he walks the Revolutionary Road
       Having found the Communist Party!

       He's joined the army and taken a vow:
       To uproot exploitation wherever it can be found.

In a hundred battles, he's passed through life and death,
While his achievements truly astound.
Many times he's used his wits to blow up enemy forts,
And saved numerous comrades and neighbors
From bandit lairs all around.
Plunging into this sea of trees,
He's often fought bandits when they arrive,
Trapping Lwan Ping, seizing Hu Byau,
And capturing Howling Wolf alive.
If I send him into the midst of danger
I'm sure his heart – flaming red
His determination – like steel
Will help him overcome Mountain Vulture
And survive.

Enter SHEN DE HWA *who goes into the house*

SHEN   Chief of Staff!

SHAU   Comrade De Hwa, how did the Democratic Meeting go?

SHEN   Everyone studied the enemy's situation in detail. We all realize
that we can only take them by strategy, not by a full offensive.
We must send a comrade who can get into the midst of the
bandits . . .

SHAU   Right. Come, let's talk about it!

Enter YANG DZ RUNG *who goes into the house.* SHAU *looks him
over carefully while* SHEN DE HWA *stares in surprise*

YANG   Hu Byan is here to present the map. *Gives the bandit salute*

SHAU   Hu Byau? Old Yang, Ha, ha, ha, ha!

SHEN   Old Yang!

YANG   Ha! Ha! Ha! Ha! *Sits down*

SHAU   Quick – tell me your idea!

YANG Chief of Staff, I think the best method of attacking Tiger Mountain is by using strategy.

SHAU Right.

YANG The enemy's Hundred Chickens Feast is a good opportunity.

SHAU Have you found out all the details?

YANG Yes, we have. Every lunar year, on the last evening of the last month, Mountain Vulture celebrates his birthday. They use chickens extorted from a hundred families and call it the Hundred Chickens Feast. *Gets up* I suggest we send a comrade right into the enemy's midst and have him find out everything about the fortress and tunnel system. Then we could take advantage of the Hundred Chickens Feast. When all the bandits are assembled in Tiger Hall, get them drunk and . . .

SHAU The pursuit detachment can spring up Tiger Mountain and attack them before they realize it!

YANG Exactly! Chief of Staff, please let me do the job!

SHEN The comrades all suggested that Old Yang could take on the responsibility!

SHAU Well, all right! Comrade De Hwa. *Hands him the Agent's Map* Take this map and make a copy of it. Uh – and notify the others that a Party Branch Meeting will be held.

SHEN Yes sir! *Exits*

SHAU Old Yang, you'll have to disguise yourself as a bandit and make your way into Tiger Mountain. Are you confident you can do it?

YANG There are three favorable conditions.

SHAU The first?

YANG Horse Cudgel Syu and the Nipple Mountain gang have just been defeated. I could pose as his cavalry adjutant, Hu Byau.

This man is now in our hands and Mountain Vulture has never seen him; moreover, I know the bandit passwords so I wouldn't give myself away.

SHAU The second?

YANG I'll give the Agent's Map to Mountain Vulture as a present on our first meeting. That will certainly earn his confidence.

SHAU Good.

YANG But the third condition is the most important. . . .

SHAU And that's the bravery of the Chinese People's Liberation Army and its loyalty to the Party and Chairman Mao!

YANG *in a heartfelt manner*
Chief of Staff, you understand me completely!

SHAU *with deep emotion*
Old Yang, this is no ordinary responsibility!

YANG Chief of Staff!

Sings

A Communist is always ready
To heed the Party's call
And take the heaviest burden upon himself.
I'm determined to smash the chains of a thousand years,
And open up an eternal spring of happiness for all.

I know I'll travel a dangerous road,
No more need be said.
For the more dangerous it is,
The more I'll forge ahead.
Raging winds and thickening clouds
May try to block my way,
But Revolutionary Wisdom can overcome
Heaven in its stead.

With the will of the old fool who was able to move mountains
I'll break through the Pass of Obstacles in one blow.
The flames raging in this Red heart of mine shall forge a sharp
          sword
To cut down the foe.

SHAU Good! You can ride Horse Cudgel Syu's black-maned horse.
      Follow the path that Hunter Chang pointed out going north-
      east . . .

YANG And wind my way up the mountain.

SHAU After you leave, the pursuit detachment will occupy Jya Pi
      Valley, mobilize the masses and prepare for the coming battle.
      We'll be waiting for your report!

YANG I'll place the report in the pine trees on the southwest side of
      Tiger Mountain. The tree will be marked the way we agreed.

SHAU I'll send Shen De Hwa to pick up the report on the twenty-sixth
      of this month.

YANG I promise you it will be sent.

SHAU Good. When the pursuit detachment receives the report, we'll
      start out immediately. From within and without, Mountain Vul-
      ture and his gang will be destroyed on Tiger Mountain!

YANG Chief of Staff, this is a well thought-out battle plan. Its settled,
      then!

SHAU *excitedly grips* YANG DZ RUNG's *arms. Pauses*
      Comrade Dz Rung! Have courage, be careful!

      Sings

      I feel certain you can bear this heavy responsibility.
      Everything depends on how it's carried out.

We'll call a Party Branch Meeting to air any doubt.
And use collective wisdom to defeat the enemy.

YANG DZ RUNG *and* SHAU JYAN PWO *grasp hands tightly and strike a martial pose*

SCENE 5   Killing a Tiger

Several days later. At the foothills of Tiger Mountain, the snow lies deep, covering the thick forest. Tall, sturdy pines reach up to the clouds while rays of sunlight pierce through the trees.

YANG   *intrepidly sings offstage*
Sweeping through a sea of trees,
Cascading over fields of snow,
My spirit rushes into the Milky Way.

YANG *enters in disguise. Whip in hand, he urges his horse onward. In a series of dances, he pierces through the deep forest, leaps across mountain streams, climbs up towering peaks, descends along steep slopes, gallops across a wide expanse and then stops to look out in all directions*

Sings

I erupt with martial vigor,
I issue forth brave determination,
Facing the mountains, all this I display.

Let the Red Flag fly throughout the world.
Charge across boiling seas, razor cliffs – why mind?
How I long to change the snow to a flowing stream,
And welcome a new Spring for all mankind!

The Party gives me wisdom and courage, too.
A thousand trials, ten thousand dangers count as but a few.

To eradicate the bandits I must first pose as one.
Into Tiger Mountain, a sharp knife cuts its way through.

I swear I'll bury Mountain Vulture
In rocky valley grave.
My determination shakes these peaks.
My bravery jolts the deep ravine.
Wait until the Hundred Chickens Feast,
My comrades and I will join their conclave.
We'll upset Heaven and overturn Earth,
And wipe these bandits from the scene.

The roar of a tiger is heard in the distance. It startles the horse which stumbles. YANG, *grasping the reins, rears it, turns around, halts, and jumps down. The tiger's roar draws closer.* YANG *quickly leads the horse off. Reenters, takes off his overcoat, draws his pistol and fires at the tiger. The animal screams, then falls dead. In the distance, other shots are heard*

YANG *immediately alerted*
Shots! The bandits must be coming down the mountain. *Calmly* I just shot one down and now here comes a whole pack! I'll see that you all wind up the same way!

The BANDIT CHIEF OF STAFF *calls from offstage: 'Halt!' Enter* BANDIT CHIEF OF STAFF *leading a group of bandits.* YANG *puts his overcoat back on, stands erect and salutes the bandits*

BANDIT
CHIEF OF
STAFF 'On what road do mushrooms journey? What do they cost?' *

YANG *holding his head high, refuses to answer*

BANDIT *discovering the tiger that* YANG *has shot, cries out*
A tiger! A tiger!

The bandits all step back in fear

* Various passwords in the form of riddles are supposed to be exchanged.

YANG   Ha! Ha! Ha! Ha! You're all pretty brave, aren't you? It's just a dead tiger.

BANDIT   *looks over the animal cautiously*
What a shot! Right through the head!

BANDIT
CHIEF OF
STAFF   Did you shoot it?

YANG   He got in the way of my bullet.

BANDIT
CHIEF OF
STAFF   Hm, you're quite a fellow. Which mountain are you from and what are you doing here?

YANG   *seizing the initiative*
You look like you're from Tiger Mountain.

BANDIT
CHIEF OF
STAFF   Ha, ha! Obviously. *Realizes he gave himself away*
Huh! Where are you really from?

YANG   That's not for you to ask. I want to see Brigadier Tswei personally. I've got something important to discuss with him.

BANDIT
CHIEF OF
STAFF   How come you don't know any of the mountain rules? You're not a fellow-bandit, you're a fake!

YANG   If I were a fake would I dare to barge into Tiger Mountain like this?

BANDIT
CHIEF OF
STAFF   *menacingly*
Who sent you here? Who sent you here?

YANG *stiffens, his mind made up. He looks proudly ahead and does not answer.*

BANDITS Speak up!

YANG *proudly*
Don't ask me anything until I've seen Brigadier Tswei.

BANDIT
CHIEF OF
STAFF *powerless*
All right! Let's go! Where's your gun?

YANG Don't worry!

YANG DZ RUNG *throws his pistol to a bandit. He points to the tiger, then to the horse*

BANDIT
CHIEF OF
STAFF Carry the tiger and bring his horse.

BANDITS Yes sir!

YANG DZ RUNG *freezes in a martial pose. Resolute, and calm, he boldly walks ahead*

SCENE 6 Into the Bandits' Stronghold

Immediately follows the previous act. Inside Tiger Hall – a dark mountain cave lit by several lamps hung about. MOUNTAIN VULTURE *sits in a chair. The* EIGHT INVINCIBLES *stand about him on each side. A group of petty bandits stand in back of the hall, to the left.* MOUNTAIN VULTURE *commands the* BANDIT CHIEF OF STAFF *to bring in the captive*

CHIEF OF
STAFF Third Brother's order! Bring in *Lyou dz!*

BANDITS Bring in *Lyou dz!*

Enter YANG DZ RUNG, *his head held high*

YANG *sings*
Though I've come alone to this dragon's pool, this tiger's den
My class brothers stand beside me, a million men.
Let Mountain Vulture burn and pillage for miles around, then!
It only strengthens my fighting spirit –
To go forth for the People against these devils again!

YANG *goes forward and proudly salutes the bandits*

MOUNTAIN
VULTURE *challenges him*
'The King of Heaven has cornered the Earthly Tiger.'

YANG 'The Precious Pagoda suppresses the River Demon.'

INVINCIBLES *Moha? Moha?*

YANG 'When I spoke at noon, no one was home.'

MOUNTAIN
VULTURE 'Why is your face so red?'

YANG 'My spirit is in flames.'

MOUNTAIN
VULTURE 'How come it's become yellow again?'

The bandits grasp their swords and close in about him

YANG *calmly*
'I smeared it with wax against the cold.'

MOUNTAIN VULTURE *draws his gun and shoots out a lamp.* YANG
takes a gun from the CHIEF OF STAFF *and shoots out two lamps.*
The bandits whisper among themselves but are silenced by the
INVINCIBLES

MOUNTAIN
VULTURE   Uh, from what you say, you must be one of Commander Syu's men.

YANG   I'm Hu Byau, Commander Syu's Cavalry Adjutant.

MOUNTAIN
VULTURE   Hu Byau? Then tell me, when did you join up with Commander Syu?

YANG   When he became Chief of Police.

MOUNTAIN
VULTURE   I hear there are several things Commander Syu is fond of.

YANG   Two treasures.

MOUNTAIN
VULTURE   Which two treasures?

YANG   A fast horse and a quick-slicing sword.

MOUNTAIN
VULTURE   What is his horse like?

YANG   It has curly hair and a black mane.

VULTURE   What is his sword like?

YANG   It's a Japanese commander's sword.

MOUNTAIN
VULTURE   Who gave it to him?

YANG   The Imperial Japanese Army.

MOUNTAIN
VULTURE   Where?

YANG   In the Hall of Five Unities by the Peony River.

MOUNTAIN
VULTURE *pauses*

Hmm . . . well, if you're Commander Syu's Cavalry Adjutant, last time Commissioner Hou called a meeting, how come I saw Adjutant Lwan Ping there and not you?

YANG Brigadier, I'm just a straggling foot-soldier of Commander Syu's. How can I compare to Lwan Ping? He's the one who appears on all the important occasions.

MOUNTAIN
VULTURE Just why did you come to Tiger Mountain?

YANG I've come to join up with you, Brigadier, and make a name for myself. Today, I've just barely crossed your threshold and all the elder brothers here mistrust me – isn't this against our code of brotherhood?

MOUNTAIN
VULTURE Ha, Ha, Ha. Why . . . that's only for the protection of our fortress here.

INVINCIBLES Ha! Ha! Ha! Ha!

MOUNTAIN
VULTURE Hu Byau, when was Nipple Mountain captured?

YANG During the last month of the year, on the third day.

MOUNTAIN
VULTURE Then how could you have kept on traveling for so many days?

YANG Brigadier, it was quite easy for me. When Nipple Mountain fell, I fled to White Pine Bay and hid there for a few days.

MOUNTAIN
VULTURE White Pine Bay?

YANG At the home of Lwan Ping's uncle.

MOUNTAIN
VULTURE Did you see Lwan Ping?

YANG Yes, I did.

MOUNTAIN
VULTURE And Howling Wolf?

YANG Howling Wolf?

MOUNTAIN
VULTURE Uh.

YANG I don't know about him.

MOUNTAIN
VULTURE Hu Byau, *you've* come here but why didn't Lwan Ping come too?

YANG Lwan Ping?

MOUNTAIN
VULTURE Yes.

YANG Oh, better not to bring it up!

MOUNTAIN
VULTURE What?

YANG Well, I . . . *Glances around at the group of bandits*

MOUNTAIN VULTURE *gives a command and the bandits leave*

MOUNTAIN
VULTURE Hu Byau, what's all this about Adjutant Lwan?

YANG It's hard to say in a few words!

Sings

When I think of Lwan Ping,
My anger is hard to suppress –

MOUNTAIN
  VULTURE What happened?

    YANG *sings*
Throughout the countryside, Brotherhood should come first
But of that he couldn't have cared less!

MOUNTAIN
  VULTURE What? How come he ignored the feelings of Brotherhood?

    YANG *continues to sing*
Both of us were saved by luck when Nipple Mountain fell.
I urged him to change associates –
At Tiger Mountain we'd do well.

MOUNTAIN
  VULTURE Was he going to come or not?

    YANG *continues to sing*
Every man has his ambition,
One cannot be forced.
But he shouldn't have –
He shouldn't have spoken so recklessly,
Without the least remorse.

MOUNTAIN
  VULTURE What did he say?

    YANG He said . . .

MOUNTAIN
  VULTURE What did he say?

    YANG Uh . . .

MOUNTAIN
  VULTURE *extremely agitated*
Eh, Old Hu, speak up – tell me quickly!

YANG He said –

Continues to sing

Mountain Vulture has to jump
At Commissioner Hou's . . .

MOUNTAIN
VULTURE What?

YANG . . . commands.

MOUNTAIN
VULTURE What? I jump at his commands?

INVINCIBLES Damn him! He must be joking!

YANG Lwan Ping had some more to say.

INVINCIBLES What else?

YANG *sings*
The Eight Invincibles are
A worthless pack of rats.

INVINCIBLES *full of rage, shout*
Hah! That scheming devil!

YANG *sings*
He calls himself a Phoenix on a search.
Seeking the highest branch on which to perch.
Commissioner Hou's roots spread deeply –
Like a mammoth, mountain-firm tree.

INVINCIBLES To Hell with him!

YANG *continues to sing*
While speaking he drew out a map.

MOUNTAIN
VULTURE A map?

YANG *sings*
A map all rolled up.

MOUNTAIN VULTURE, *with a greedy look in his face, prances around* YANG

YANG *sings*
He was going over to the Commissioner
to present the map and earn a promotion.

MOUNTAIN
VULTURE Was it the Agent's Map?

YANG Yes, it was that secret Agent's Map.

MOUNTAIN
VULTURE You mean he gave that map to Commissioner Hou?

YANG Don't get so excited.

Continues to sing, smiling sarcastically

Gloating, he grinned 'til nearly out of his mind
And from inside brought out –

– A jar of wine.
Bowl after bowl, I poured him a flood.
Lwan Ping got so drunk
He flopped down just like mud!

INVINCIBLES Ha! Ha! He got drunk!

YANG I figured he was so drunk he couldn't move . . .

MOUNTAIN
VULTURE Ah hah!

YANG So I . . .

MOUNTAIN
VULTURE Killed him!

YANG Oh no, I couldn't – we were friends for many years!

MOUNTAIN
  VULTURE Ah . . . *Changes his manner* That's right! Friendship is important, very important! Old Hu, what did you do then?

YANG He had his plans but I had my own.

MOUNTAIN
  VULTURE And . . . ?

YANG I . . .

MOUNTAIN
  VULTURE Ah?

YANG *continues to sing*
  Switching into his clothes before he could know,
  I jumped on the black-maned horse,
  And through the billowing snow,
  Rushed up to Tiger Mountain in one breath.

MOUNTAIN
  VULTURE Old Hu, you mean you've got hold of the Agent's Map?

YANG *laughing lightly*
  Ha, ha, ha, ha.

  Sings

  Brigadier – raise your head and take a look
  The precious map is in front of your eyes!

  Unrolls the map. YANG *stands above the bandits looking down on them as* MOUNTAIN VULTURE *formally shakes his sleeves and receives the map. He looks at it as the group of bandits crowd around*

MOUNTAIN
VULTURE *sings*
Agent's Map! Morning and night
You've been on my mind.
Today at last my heart can unwind!

Laughs wildly

Ha! Ha! Ha! Ha!

INVINCIBLES Old Hu is really something! Good going!

YANG *suggestively*
Brigadier, with the Agent's Map in your hands, the entire Peony River area will be ours!

MOUNTAIN
VULTURE Right, right! Old Hu's right! When the Nationalist Armies come, I'll be a commander. You can all become brigadiers and division commanders.

INVINCIBLES We all depend on your generosity, Chief!

YANG *laughing coldly*
Ha, ha, ha.

MOUNTAIN
VULTURE Old Hu, you've been a great help to Tiger Mountain. I'm going to name you 'Old Ninth.'

YANG Thanks, Chief!

MOUNTAIN
VULTURE We're members of the Nationalist Army so you ought to have a title. I appoint you full Colonel and Deputy Regimental Commander of the Fifth Peace Preservation Brigade of the Eastern Heilungjyang Region.

YANG *mounts the platform*
Thank you, Third Brother, for the promotion! From now on I'll depend on all my elder brothers for guidance!

INVINCIBLES Well said! Well said!

CHIEF OF
  STAFF Bring some wine!

Enter bandits who distribute wine to all

Let's drink a toast to Old Ninth and his glorious promotion!

MOUNTAIN
  VULTURE For delivering the Agent's Map and triumphing over such hardship!

YANG *bravely sings*
How it pains me today to drink their wine.
While my great ambition remains unfulfilled
I shall not rest.
The day will come when my skill shall shine.
I'll drink to them now and later write this down
In blood as protest!

YANG *drains the winecup, wearing a triumphant smile*

YANG *fearlessly*
Ha! Ha! Ha!

SCENE 7 Arousing the Masses

Jyapi Valley. Inside and outside the house of LI YUNG CHI. *Noon.
The wind and snow rage*

MOTHER LI *sings*
Illness racks my body.
Our food supply is gone.
I call to my son
But there's no one to respond.

When will the poor get revenge
For debts of blood and tears?

Enter JANG DA SHAN

JANG Aunt!

MOTHER LI Is it Da Shan?

JANG *enters the house*

JANG Aunt, are you feeling better today?

MOTHER LI This morning, when I got up, I was even dizzier than before.

JANG Aunt, I brought these tubers . . . *Hands her the roots*

MOTHER LI *anxiously receiving them*
Da Shan – again you brought . . .

JANG Aunt, though Yung Chi isn't here, we're still one big family!

JANG *heats some water.* MOTHER LI *brings the tubers into the house.* LI YUNG CHI, *his face now full-bearded, quickly enters wearing tattered clothes. He pushes open the door and goes into the house*

JANG *startled*
Yung Chi!

LI Da Shan!

MOTHER LI *comes forward from the back of the house*

MOTHER LI Yung . . . Chi!

Sings

Can I be dreaming that you should arrive?
But no – those bruises are real – they make my heart ache.
How did you escape from the tiger's mouth . . .

. . . alive?

LI *continues to sing*
In the back of the mountain
There was a high cliff.
I jumped and escaped down
A perilous road.

MOTHER LI *sings*
Mother and son meet again in a
Blend of joy and pain.
The happier I am the more I still think
Of those two who were slain.

LI How many hatreds are branded on my heart?
It fills my breast with fiery rage.
The day will come to fight, struggle,
And tear our enemies apart.

A crowd of people shout 'Soldiers are entering the village.' PLA
fighters shout 'Neighbors, do not flee! We're with you!

JANG Ah, has Mountain Vulture struck again?

LI Have they come to get me?

JANG You'd better hide quickly while I go out and have a look.

JANG *pulls out a dagger and exits*

MOTHER LI Hide somewhere, son!

LI Hide? Mother, just where am I going to hide? Its better to rush
out and fight them now! I'll break even if I get one of them and
if I get two, I'll be one ahead!

MOTHER LI Yung Chi . . . you'd . . .

Enter JUNG JR CHENG *and* LYU HUNG YE

LYU *knocks at the door*
Are there any of you neighbors inside?

LI   Yes! We're not dead yet!

LYU   Old Neighbor!

JUNG   Aunt!

LI YUNG CHI opens the door forcefully. JUNG JR CHENG and LYU HUNG YE enter the house. JUNG closes the door. This startles MOTHER LI who goes to protect LI YUNG CHI

LYU   Don't be afraid, Aunt. We're . . .

LI   Come to the point!

LYU   *to LI YUNG CHI*
Neighbor, we're from the Chinese People's Liberation Army.

LI   *studies them carefully*
Hah! This 'army,' that 'army,' I've seen too many of you. Who knows which army you belong to. If you've got anything on your mind, say it now! Do you want money? We haven't got any! Do you want food? You people already stolen it! Do you want my life . . . ?

MOTHER LI   Yung Chi!

JUNG   Neighbor, we're worker and peasant soldiers. We protect the people.

LI   *sarcastically*
That sounds just fine!

MOTHER LI becomes dizzy

LI   Mother!

LYU   *To JUNG JR CHENG*
Aunt isn't feeling well. We'll go find someone to come and have a look at her.

JUNG Good.

LI You can't fool me! *He helps* MOTHER LI *to the back of the house*

JUNG JR CHENG gives a signal to LYU HUNG YE *and both leave the hut, closing the door behind them. Enter* SHAU JYAN PWO *and* LITTLE GWO

JUNG Chief of Staff!

SHAU How are things going?

LYU There's an old lady in the house who is sick.

SHAU Oh? Order a medic sent here quickly – tell her to bring along some food.

LYU Yes sir! *Exits*

JUNG It's sure tough working with the masses here.

SHAU The neighbors here in Jyapi Valley don't seem to understand us. They've been deceived by the bandits. You've forgotten, but didn't Howling Wolf pass himself off as one of our reconnaissance men?

JUNG Right.

SHAU Little Jung, if we don't arouse the masses we won't be able to get a firm foothold and eliminate Mountain Vulture. But if we don't smash those bandits first, the masses can never truly be aroused.

JUNG *laughs*
I understand.

SHAU Go and tell everyone: We must concern ourselves with the Peoples troubles, patiently spread word of the Party's policies, sternly uphold the Three Rules of Discipline and the Eight Points of Attention so that we can deal with the situation practically.

JUNG Yes sir! *Turns and is about to leave*

SHAU Oh – and ask around and see if Hunter Chang has arrived or not.

JUNG Yes sir! *Exits*

Enter MEDICAL ORDERLY

ORDERLY Chief of Staff! *Hands him a sack of grain* Where is the patient?

SHAU In this house. *Points to the Li home*

ORDERLY Neighbors! *Knocks at the door*

SHAU Neighbors, our doctor has arrived. Open up, quickly!

> LI YUNG CHI *angrily rushes onstage grasping a dagger.* MOTHER
> LI *follows, trying to stop him*

MOTHER LI Yung Chi . . . don't . . .

LI What are you afraid of? This is enough to fight them with!

He sticks the dagger into the table

MOTHER LI Yung Chi – I beg you! *She faints*

LI *quickly holds her up*
Ma! Ma!

> SHAU *forces the door open and enters with the* MEDICAL ORDERLY
> *and* LITTLE GWO. LI YUNG CHI *glares at* SHAU *while protecting*
> MOTHER LI

SHAU Quickly – try to save her!

ORDERLY Yes sir!

> SHAU *takes off his coat and wraps it around* MOTHER LI. *The*
> MEDICAL ORDERLY *helps* MOTHER LI *enter the backroom.* LI YUNG
> CHI *and* LITTLE GWO *follow them inside*

SHAU *takes some grain from the foodbag and puts it in a pot to boil. After a while,* LI YUNG CHI *comes out for some water.* SHAU *enters the backroom*

LI   *discovering gruel in the pot, he is deeply moved and ponders*
From the Chinese People's Liberation Army?

Sings

The soldiers hurry to cure our sick and keep us alive.
They brave the cold to bring us warmth.
Soldiers and bandits worked always together,
Oppressing the people so none could survive.
But today my clouds of doubt are beginning to disperse!

Are you really the saving star we've all been waiting for?

MOTHER LI   *cries from the back of the house*
Water!

LI YUNG CHI *pours out some of the gruel.* LITTLE GWO *comes out from inside, gets the gruel and goes back in.* SHAU *comes out of the backroom*

SHAU   Old Neighbor, she's come to. Don't worry. What's your name?

LI   Li Yung Chi.

SHAU   Are you a native of this place?

LI   No, I'm from Shandung. My father was a worker in Jinan but after the April 12 Coup, he went on strike one day and was killed by Chiang Kai-shek's men . . .

SHAU   *showing anger and sympathy*
Huh! *Warmly* Then how did you come here?

LI   After my father died, my mother brought us here to the Northeast.

SHAU   How do you live?

LI   I'm a railroad worker.

SHAU   *excitedly*
Good! Then you're one of us!

LI   *carefully looking over* SHAU JYAN PWO
What kind of troops are you really? What are you doing here deep in the mountains?

SHAU   *warmly*
Old Neighbor! *Sings*

We're the army of peasants and workers,
Through these deep mountains we've tread,
To destroy all reactionaries, to change Heaven and Earth.
For decades, North and South,
The Revolution has spread.
The Communist Party and Chairman Mao lead us forward!

A Red Star on our caps.
The Red Flag of Revolution pinned on our collars.
Wherever it flies, dark clouds disperse.
In liberated areas, people overthrow
Their landlords and start life anew.
The People's Army and the People together
Suffer hardships through.
We've come to sweep out all bandits
And give Tiger Mountain its due!

LI   *like spring thunder, his feelings burst forth as he sings*
Our eyes were exhausted,
Searching for you night and day.
Who thought we could
Fight the bandits,
Pierce through deep mountains,
Rescue the poor,
Cast off our hardships,
Or that our own army would come this way!

Resolutely sings

Friends – I should have separated black and white
And distinguished right from wrong.
Taking my friends as foes –
I've felt ashamed all along.

He pushes over the dagger that was stuck in the table

For thirty years I've worked like a horse,
With never a day of bliss.
Bearing scars and bruises,
Its hard to suppress my rage
While I struggle in a bottomless abyss.
We suffer here in untold anguish,
Full of pain and fury.
All of it directed against
The bandits on Tiger Mountain.
Many said these bitter years
Would last as long as we could forsee.
Who would have expected that today
Withered branches have sprouted and
Blossoms appeared on an iron tree.

From now on I'll follow the Party
And drive out those wolves with a thirst.
Fire and Water won't hold me back.
If they crush my body and break all my bones,
Through a thousand trials and ten thousand dangers,
To sweep clean Tiger Mountain
I'll still be there first!

SHAU JYAN PWO *grasps* LI YUNG CHI'S *hand.* LYU HUNG YE *calls from offstage: 'Chief of Staff!' and enters*

LYU The villagers have all come to see you!

A throng of villagers and soldiers enter. The MEDICAL ORDERLY *helps* MOTHER LI *out of the backroom*

VILLAGER Chief Officer . . .

SOLDIER Old man, we don't use those terms. Call him 'Commander.'

SHAU *quickly*
Just call me comrade.

JUNG Chief of Staff, this is Old Chang.

SHAU *goes forward to shake* HUNTER CHANG's *hand*
Old Chang, have you come here from the forest?

HUNTER
CHANG We couldn't live by the mountain any more. I've come with my child to move in with her Uncle Da Shan.

SHAU *pats* CHANG BAU
Good girl!

LI Old Brother Chang!

HUNTER
CHANG Yung Chi, our saving star has come at last.

JANG Commander, the hearts of everyone in this village are burning with one desire – to attack Tiger Mountain!

SHAU Neighbors! Our Chinese People's Liberation Army has scored a great victory at the front! The entire Peony River area has been liberated!

VILLAGERS Hurrah!

SHAU Mountain Vulture has nowhere to run!

JANG Let's go stir up his nest!

LI Commander, please issue us some rifles!

VILLAGERS Right! Give us guns!

LI If we only had guns, anyone in Jya Pi Valley could bring down two or three of those bandits!

SHAU We'll certainly issue guns to everyone! But just now you don't have any warm winter clothes and everybody is short of grain. How can you go into the deep mountains and fight bandits?

VILLAGERS What can we do?

SHAU There are medicinal herbs growing all around here and a mountainload of timber. If we can get the train to run, couldn't we trade them for food and clothing?

VILLAGERS That's right!

SHAU If we organize everyone into a People's Militia, we can certainly get the train through. Then we'll have something to eat and something to wear. And when we fight Mountain Vulture, we'll be all the stronger!

LI When can we start work repairing the railroad?

SHAU Why not now? Let's all work together!

VILLAGER Commander, this is heavy labor!

JUNG Old man, we're all from poor families. When we pick up our guns, we fight. When we get hold of some tools, we work!

LI *runs to* SHAU JYAN PWO *and excitedly grasps his hand*
Great! Commander, we're all one big family!

Sings

When mountain people speak,
They mean what they say.
With one true heart,
We can deal with the world!
To catch a dragon
We'll go with you . . .

VILLAGERS . . . under the sea.

LI *continues singing*
To fight a tiger . . .

VILLAGERS . . . we'll follow you up tall mountains!

LI A clap of spring thunder
Shakes Heaven and Earth!
Mountain Vulture!

VILLAGERS
AND
SOLDIERS *sing*
Now let's see how long you live!

Soldiers and people crowd together and strike a fierce, martial pose

SCENE 8 Sending Out a Report

Dawn. An open space near the top of Tiger Mountain. A group of forts can be seen among the crags. Mountains in the background, all under heavy snow. To the right lies the main road leading down from the mountain

MOUNTAIN
VULTURE Is this where Old Ninth often comes to exercise?

BANDIT
CHIEF OF
STAFF Yes.

MOUNTAIN
VULTURE Where else has he been?

BANDIT
CHIEF OF
STAFF He's been to have a look at all the forts on our five peaks.

MOUNTAIN
VULTURE What! You let him see our nine groups of twenty-seven forts?

BANDIT
CHIEF OF
STAFF He's one of the brothers now, so I thought he should see the place.

MOUNTAIN
VULTURE Hah! I don't like what's been going on in the last few days — there's been some movement at the foot of the mountain. Howling Wolf's gone and still not back. Nobody's heard of Hu Byau before this. He just happens to show up now — I have to be on guard!

BANDIT CHIEF ADJUTANT *enters from right*

BANDIT
CHIEF
ADJUTANT Third Brother, it's all been arranged according to your orders.

MOUNTAIN
VULTURE Good, then carry it out the way we said last night. Let's prick him and see if he shows any blood!

BANDIT
CHIEF
ADJUTANT Right *Exits to the right*

MOUNTAIN VULTURE *and* BANDIT CHIEF OF STAFF *see somebody approaching and leave quickly to the left*

YANG *sings from offstage*
Hacking my way through thistles and thorns,
I struggle . . .

Enters

. . . in the heart of the enemy!

Gazing far off
I think of my comrades.
Army and People joining hands,
awaiting the signal to attack these wolves.
Meanwhile my fighting-spirit expands!

The Party placed their hopes on me.
The Comrades gave me their best advice.
Heavy words reaching from the heart,
Exhorting me to sacrifice.
A red fire rages in my heart,
Warming my breast through snow and ice.

One must possess great courage,
Yet have caution engraved upon the heart.
Depend on bravery,
Yet develop strategy into an art.
The Party's word is Victory's guarantee,
For Mao Tse-tung's Thought shines gloriously!

Tiger Mountain has layers of defenses,
Forts above and tunnels below.
The Leadership feels we could win using strategy
And all that we know.
But in a headlong attack
We'd suffer a heavy blow.

After seven days amongst the enemy
I know them like the back of my hand.
Concealed on my person is
A report of their situation.
I'll send it out at dawn,
Pretending to take a walk, as planned.

Notices something

Why have they increased the guards about here
– I don't understand!

This report . . .
This report must go out

Or this chance will flee.
The great plan will be spoiled.
I'll let down the People.
I'll let down the Party.

New Year's Eve approaches fast.
I mustn't long remain.
Though the grass be knives,
And the trees, swords
I'll face ten thousand difficulties
To get down this mountain.

Ice and snow melt, the cold is outdone,
For in my heart burns the morning sun!

Brightness fills the misty sky as a ray of sunlight tinges the crags with red. Voices from backstage call: 'Hurry up! Let's go!' 'All right, I'm coming!' YANG *is alerted, takes off his coat and pretends to be exercising. Two bandits enter and pretend to be on patrol. They call to* YANG

BANDITS Eh, Ninth Brother! Morning!

YANG Morning!

Both BANDITS *exit.* YANG *prepares to go. Gunshots sound in the distance*

YANG Shooting!

Heard in the distance: 'Charge!' 'Kill!' Heard closer by: 'The Communists have come!' The shooting increases

YANG What? Have the comrades come already? *He thinks, then decides* The Chief of Staff hasn't received my report. He couldn't have come at this time.

The shooting becomes more intense as the shouts come nearer

YANG Those rifle shots don't sound quite right! Ah hah! Another test! I'll take care of their trick with one of my own. Then I'll send the report off. *He fires into the air twice, then yells to the left* Brothers!

Enter four BANDITS

YANG The Communist Army has come! Come with me and attack them!

The four bandits exit. MOUNTAIN VULTURE, BANDIT CHIEF OF STAFF *secretly enter. The* BANDIT CHIEF ADJUTANT *comes forward*

MOUNTAIN
VULTURE Old Ninth, Old Ninth, hold off!

YANG *shouting to the right*
Halt where you are!

BANDIT
CHIEF OF
STAFF *calls to the right at the same time*
Don't shoot! Don't shoot!

Bandits call from offstage: 'Right!'

YANG *to* MOUNTAIN VULTURE
What?

MOUNTAIN
VULTURE Hah! This was a military exercise I set up!

YANG Why, if you hadn't stopped me in time, I would have plugged them full of holes!

MOUNTAIN
VULTURE Ha! Ha! Ha! Ha!

YANG Third Brother, how come you didn't tell Old Ninth you were setting up a military exercise? You should have . . .

MOUNTAIN
VULTURE   Eh, Old Ninth, don't get upset. This time I didn't tell anyone about the exercise – ask him. *Points to the* CHIEF ADJUTANT

BANDIT
CHIEF
ADJUTANT   *pretentiously*
Why yes, that's true. Even *I* thought the Communists were coming.

YANG   Ha! Ha! *Insinuatingly* Let them come! I'll be waiting for them!

MOUNTAIN
VULTURE   Old Ninth, You're all right! Ha! Ha! Ha!

BANDIT
CAPTAIN   *from offstage*
Come on, move it!

The CAPTAIN *pushes a bandit onstage. The* BANDIT *falls to the ground*

BANDIT
CAPTAIN   Third Brother, here's a fake who bumped into the wall outside.

MOUNTAIN
VULTURE   What?

BANDIT   *trembling with fear*
Third Brother, we went down the mountain as ordered and saw the railroad running in the distance. We couldn't even get into Jya Pi Valley before we ran into the Communist Army!

MOUNTAIN
VULTURE   Jya Pi Valley? *Suspiciously*
And you're the only one who made it back?

BANDIT   Yes.

MOUNTAIN
VULTURE   The Communists captured all of you and let only you return?

BANDIT   No! No!

MOUNTAIN
VULTURE   You bastard! *Picks up a gun and points it at the bandit*

YANG   *stopping him*
          Third Brother, why shoot him? If he really had been taken prisoner by the Communists would he have dared return?

BANDIT
CHIEF OF
STAFF   Sure, everybody knows Third Brother hates anyone who lets the Communists capture him!

MOUNTAIN
VULTURE   Hah!

YANG   *to the bandit*
          Get out of here, you're making Third Brother angry!

BANDIT
CHIEF OF
STAFF   *kicks the bandit*
          Beat it!

BANDIT   *walking off to one side, in a low voice*
          Old Ninth is a good fellow. *Exits*

BANDIT
CHIEF OF
STAFF   *to the* BANDIT CAPTAIN
          Send an order down below to tighten our fortifications.

BANDIT
CAPTAIN   Yes sir! *Exits*

MOUNTAIN
VULTURE   *in low spirits*
          Eh!

BANDIT
CHIEF OF
STAFF   Third Brother, I'll send some men down the mountain on a raid. They'll capture something and we can all celebrate at the Hundred Chickens Feast!

MOUNTAIN
VULTURE   All right, but this time, I want them to be especially careful!

BANDIT
CHIEF OF
STAFF   I know. *Exits*

YANG   Third Brother, with the defenses we have on Tiger Mountain, there's nothing to worry about. But why should we wait for others to attack us first?

MOUNTAIN
VULTURE   Right. What do you think we should do?

YANG   Right now, we should practice methods of attack.

MOUNTAIN
VULTURE   Hm.

YANG   And get our soldiers into good shape.

MOUNTAIN
VULTURE   Right.

YANG   After we finish eating the Hundred Chickens Feast, we can attack Jya Pi Valley!

MOUNTAIN
VULTURE   *grasping* YANG's *hand*
You're a smart fellow! Old Ninth, I'll give you command of instructing the men on how to attack.

YANG   Yes sir!

MOUNTAIN
VULTURE Ha! Ha! Ha! Ha!

Exit MOUNTAIN VULTURE *and* BANDIT CHIEF ADJUTANT

YANG *in a low voice full of contempt*
That old ass!

Sings

Mountain Vulture's quite a fool,
Playing these kinds of tricks.
For he's given me my chance
To go down the mountain.

Comrade De Hwa –

The responsibility to pick up the report falls on you.
We'll sing a song of Victory,
When the Hundred Chickens Feast comes due!

Strikes a martial pose

SCENE 9 Marching to the Attack

*The twenty-ninth day of the last month in the lunar calendar.
Morning. A spot outside the gate to* LI YUNG CHI's *house. A pair
of red scrolls bearing a New Year's couplet is pasted on the gate.
A feeling of joy and redemption prevails. As the curtain rises,
the sound of the train whistle is heard. A group of villagers of
Jya Pi Valley carrying sacks of grain on their backs, enter, smiling happily. They watch the train depart and then continue on.
One villager has been carrying a sack for Mother Li and puts it
down in front of the gate*

MOTHER LI *sings*
Soldiers and People joined as one family.

In our mountain village, a scene of joy.
A fine snow whirls as people laugh.
Dividing food and clothes, we celebrate our new lives.

Enter SHAU JYAN PWO

SHAU Aunt!

MOTHER LI Commander!

SHAU Have you enough to celebrate the New Year with?

MOTHER LI Plenty! I never dreamed we could have such a good New Year in Jya Pi Valley! If you hadn't come, I don't know how we would have made it through the year!

SHAU There are still better days to come!

MOTHER LI It's all due to the Communist Party – and the blessings of Chairman Mao!

SHAU *picks up the sack of grain and brings it inside for* MOTHER LI. *From backstage comes the sound of* LI YUNG CHI *training the People's Militia*

LI *offstage*
One! Two! Three! Four!

MILITIA *offstage*
One! Two! Three! Four!

MOTHER LI The Militia is full of energy! But the ones who are going to stay behind and defend the village have their own ideas – especially Chang Bau. She doesn't want to stay behind no matter what!

SHAU Oh, that girl . . .

MILITIA *offstage*
Kill! Kill! Kill!

SHAU and MOTHER LI continue to chat as they exit. From back-stage the voices of the Militia in training are heard again: 'Straight ahead – charge! Kill! Kill! Kill!' CHANG BAU quickly enters, still looking back at the MILITIA

CHANG BAU *sings*

As they busily train to exterminate bandits
I watch their spirit soar.
Such fire burns in my breast too
I long to join them even more.

One thought by night – one daydream,
To kill those wolves, wipe a blood debt clean.
I oil my gun and sharpen my sword,
Hatred fills me for that bandit horde.
Into the wolf's cave, the tiger's lair,
Through wind and snow, up winding hills I dare.

Why am I kept down
To guard the town?

I'll run and find the Chief of Staff
And let him know what's on my mind.
I'll insist, I'll demand to go along and fight,
And swear to wipe those bandits out of sight.

Enter MEDICAL ORDERLY

MEDICAL
ORDERLY   Chang Bau!

CHANG BAU   Sister, put in a word for me! Come on, let's find the Chief of Staff!

She pulls the MEDICAL ORDERLY along just as SHAU JYAN PWO comes out of the LI house

SHAU   Eh? What are you two talking over?

Enter LI YUNG CHI

CHANG BAU   Uncle, say I can go too!

SHAU   But protecting the village is also part of the Militia's responsibility!

CHANG BAU   Ah, I hate every bit of Mountain Vulture. I must kill him with my own hands. Why, if you don't let me go . . . how could you?

SHAU   Chang Bau! You're still young!

CHANG BAU   What? Who's young?

MEDICAL
ORDERLY   Chief of Staff, Chang Bau has class consciousness. She skis well, shoots accurately and she can help me take care of the wounded. Please let her go!

LI   Commander, this child has suffered and bears a great hatred for the bandits – say that she can go!

SHAU   Hm, you're a Militia leader and feel the same way?

LI   Yes, let's let her do it.

SHAU   Well, you all seem to be of one mind about this. All right, its settled. She can go.

CHANG BAU   Yes sir!

She goes bouncing off the stage, elated. The MEDICAL ORDERLY *follows her*

LI   Commander, the two prisoners Lwan Ping and Howling Wolf have been taken away. From the looks of things, we're going to attack Tiger Mountain soon!

SHAU   What? You're impatient, aren't you?
LI *smiles*

SHAU Oh, about that road you mentioned in the back of the mountain, based on our skiing speed, how long should it take us to reach it?

LI The back way is about eighty miles longer than going up the front of the mountain, but I think no more than a day and a night.

SHAU Good! See that the Militia makes full preparations!

LI Yes sir! *Exits*

Enter JUNG JR CHENG *and* LYU HUNG YE

LYU Chief of Staff, why are we waiting around here so long? All the comrades have reached skiing speeds which are up to standards.

JUNG The People's Militia is all organized.

LYU Moreover, the High Command has sent us reinforcements.

JUNG It seems to me that we ought to set out now. We can surely win.

SHAU Comrade, at a key moment like this, we must guard against any impulsive action.

With gravity, sings

Be patient and await orders –

JUNG Yes sir!

Exit JUNG *and* LYU

SHAU *sings*
Though I try to restrain them,
My own heart is an onrushing tide,
Difficult to stem.
The day approaches to confront the enemy
Yet Shen De Hwa has not returned –
No sight of him or of the report.
If anything has happened . . .

I have yet another resort.
The Hundred Chickens Feast is a chance we can't lose.
Li Yung Chi told of a winding road we could use.
Across dangerous peaks
We'll march to the attack,
And storm Tiger Hall by ruse.

LWO CHANG JYANG *shouts from the side and enters*

LWO   Chief of Staff, Old Shen has returned.

Enter SHEN DE HWA

SHAU   *hurries forward*
Comrade De Hwa!

SHEN   *with panting breath, hands over the report*
I'm not late am I?

SHAU   *receiving the report*
No, not at all. Go on and rest!

LWO *helps* SHEN *offstage*

SHAU   *anxiously reads the report*

'. . . in the back of the mountain lies a steep road that goes straight to Tiger Hall . . . burning torches of pine will be the signal.' Old Yang is quite a hero!

LITTLE GWO *shouts from offstage* 'Chief of Staff –' *Enter* LITTLE GWO. LI YUNG CHI *and* JANG DA SHAN *also enter together*

LITTLE GWO   Chief of Staff! A report! When the train reached West Branch River, the bridge had been destroyed. We got off the train to repair it and were suddenly attacked by the bandits. We fought them off . . .

SHAU   What about the two prisoners?

LITTLE GWO   A stray bullet killed Howling Wolf.

SHAU   And Lwan Ping?

LITTLE GWO   While we went chasing the bandits, he escaped.

SHAU   Lwan Ping escaped? *Aside* If he runs back to Tiger Mountain, he'll put Comrade Yang Dz Rung in danger and spoil our plan to exterminate the bandits.

Turning back to LITTLE GWO *and* LI YUNG CHI

Assemble the troops!

LITTLE GWO
AND
LI YUNG CHI   Yes sir! *Exit*

From far off a gong is struck and the call given to fall in

SHAU   Comrade Da Shan! You and Old Chang have the responsibility of protecting the village.

JANG
DA SHAN   Yes sir!

Enter the PURSUIT DETACHMENT, PEOPLE'S MILITIA *and other* VILLAGERS.

SHAU   Comrades! Sings
The situation has suddenly changed.
Our responsibility presses.
Every second counts – there must be no slack.
Comrades, prepare
To fly forward to the attack!
Forward march!

Changes to darkness. A snowstorm rages. The PURSUIT DETACHMENT *and* PEOPLE'S MILITIA *are led along the way by* LI YUNG CHI. *They brave the wind and plow through the snow, speeding forward. Arriving at the foot of the mountain, all take off their skis. One soldier starts climbing up and slips. Two other soldiers use rope to get up. One of these also slips but uses the rope to pull himself up again. The two then cast off the rope.* SHAU JYAN PWO *leads the rest, climbing up victoriously. When they descend along steep slopes, some soldiers roll down, others jump. Quickly and boldly, they press forward*

SCENE 10 *The Hundred Chickens Feast*

New Year's Eve in Tiger Hall. As the curtain rises the sound of 'Bring in lyou dz' *is heard. Two bandits bring* LWAN PING *onstage*

LWAN PING Third Brother.

MOUNTAIN
VULTURE Lwan Ping!

LWAN PING Yes.

MOUNTAIN
VULTURE Adjutant Lwan!

LWAN PING Third Brother.

MOUNTAIN
VULTURE What are you doing?

LWAN PING Why . . . I'm wishing Third Brother a happy birthday. Ha, ha, ha!

MOUNTAIN
VULTURE Hah! Where did you come from?

LWAN PING I . . .

MOUNTAIN
VULTURE Ah?

LWAN PING I . . .

MOUNTAIN
VULTURE Speak up!

LWAN PING I . . .

MOUNTAIN
VULTURE Out with it!

LWAN PING I'll talk, I'll talk . . . I . . . came from Commissioner Hou.

MOUNTAIN
VULTURE *laughs coldly*
So, you came from Commissioner Hou.

LWAN PING Yes.

MOUNTAIN
VULTURE Ask Old Ninth to come here!

BANDIT Yes sir! Old Ninth is wanted!

Enter YANG DZ RUNG *wearing an Officer of the Day sash*

YANG Third Brother, everything has been arranged for the feast.

MOUNTAIN
VULTURE Old Ninth, look who's here!

YANG Uh. *Startled upon seeing* LWAN PING, *he quickly controls him-self. Seizing upon the ineptness of the enemy, he decides on a battle strategy* Ah! Brother Lwan, what are you doing here? How is everything? What rank did Commissioner Hou give you for joining up with him? I, Hu Byau, wish to congratulate you on your promotion!

INVINCIBLES *mockingly*
Sure, you must be a regimental commander by now! Ha, ha, ha!

LWAN PING *is still unaware of the situation*

MOUNTAIN
VULTURE What rank did Commissioner Hou give you?

LWAN PING *recognizes* YANG DZ RUNG *in disguise, smiles viciously*
Ha, ha, you're a really good Hu Byau! Why, you're nothing
but . . .

YANG Nothing but what? *Sternly* Either I'm wrong or you are! I, Hu
Byau, was friend enough to you and always acted straightfor-
wardly. Not like you, Lwan Ping! When I urged you to join
up with Commander Tswei, you tried to drag me off to Commissioner Hou – so don't say I wasn't on the level with you!
Quickly! Answer Third Brother's question! What business
brought you here?

LWAN PING *turning away from* YANG DZ RUNG
Third Brother, let me explain . . .

YANG Quit stalling! Today we celebrate Third Brother's fiftieth birthday – there is no time to listen to your nonsense.

MOUNTAIN
VULTURE That's right! Stop beating around the bush and tell me why you
came here!

LWAN PING To join up with Third Brother's forces.

MOUNTAIN
VULTURE Hah!

YANG Then why did you try to get an appointment from Commissioner
Hou?

LWAN PING *is utterly confused and unable to answer*

YANG Listen Lwan, why did Commissioner Hou send you here? Speak
the truth!

INVINCIBLES That's right! Speak up! Speak up!

LWAN PING But I didn't come from Commissioner Hou!

BANDIT
CHIEF OF
    STAFF Huh! That's not what the bastard said a minute ago – he just
           turns away and forgets old debts! Quite a liar!

The bandits break into laughter

LWAN PING Stop laughing! You've fallen into a traitor's trap. He's not Hu
           Byau, he's in the Communist Army.

The INVINCIBLES *pull out their guns and aim at* YANG DZ RUNG

    YANG *calmly*
           Ha! Ha! Ha! Ha! Good! If you say I'm a Communist, I must be
           a Communist. Now, in front of Third Brother and the others,
           tell them about my 'Communist background!'

MOUNTAIN
  VULTURE Right! You said he wasn't Hu Byau but a Communist. How did
           you know him?

LWAN PING *stuttering*
           He . . . He . . .

  BANDITS Hah!

LWAN PING He . . .

    YANG Third Brother, this guy Lwan can only stutter and stammer. He
           rambles and contradicts himself. I think he must have some trick
           up his sleeve.

BANDIT
CHIEF OF
    STAFF I'll bet he was captured by the Communists and then set free!

LWAN PING No, no!

YANG   Did the Communists set you free or did they send you here themselves?

INVINCIBLES   Talk!

LWAN PING   I . . .

BANDIT
CHIEF
ADJUTANT   Right! The Communists sent you here, didn't they?

INVINCIBLES   Speak up! Out with it!

LWAN PING   *stares blankly ahead, tongue-tied*

YANG   Third Brother, we've fortified Tiger Mountain so that it's impregnable – the Communists have no way of breaking in. There must be some plot for them to send this bastard here.

LWAN PING   *quickly speaks up*
No, it's not true. I swear!

YANG   Lwan Ping!

Sings

This shifty fellow has hidden tricks
And stutters to conceal a traitorous scheme.
Climbing to our mountain gate,
His footprints in the snow
Leave a perfect path
For the Communist Army to follow.

Walks up the steps

Captain –

Enter BANDIT CAPTAIN

BANDIT
CAPTAIN   Yes sir!

YANG *continues singing*
Double the guard, keep a careful watch.
Without my order,
Let no one
Leave his post!

MOUNTAIN
VULTURE Right! No one leaves his post without Old Ninth's order!

BANDIT
CAPTAIN Yes sir! *Exits*

The INVINCIBLES *nod in agreement*

MOUNTAIN
VULTURE *leaves his chair and throws* LWAN PING *to the ground*
Hah! You renegade dog! First you try to drag Old Ninth to join Commissioner Hou, now you plot to divide up here and lead the Communists in. You've gone too far!

LWAN PING Third Brother, he's not Hu Byau – he's really a Communist!

YANG Lwan! You viper! *Runs down the stairs* You're trying to use Third Brother's knife to have me killed. When we were drinking at White Pine Bay, I regret I didn't take care of you with one stroke!

INVINCIBLES Right! Right!

YANG Third Brother, I've never let petty men push me around. It was for your sake that I condemn this dog yet he continues to maliciously attack me. If you think I'm in the Communist Army then deal with me right here! – If you take me for Hu Byau, then let me leave this mountain. If he stays, I go. It's either me or him. Third Brother, decide as you please! *Takes off the sash and throws it on the ground*

Mountain Vulture is stunned

BANDITS Ninth Brother can't leave us! He can't go!

INVINCIBLES Third Brother, don't let Old Ninth leave! Old Ninth, you can't go!

BANDIT
CHIEF OF
STAFF *picks up the sash and gives it to Mountain Vulture*
Third Brother, don't let him leave!

BANDITS Old Ninth, you can't leave us!

MOUNTAIN
VULTURE Uh, uh, uh, Old Ninth, you're acting like a child about this. Here, put it on, put it on. Third Brother would never treat you meanly. Ha, ha, ha, ha!

The BANDIT CHIEF OF STAFF *receives the sash from* MOUNTAIN VULTURE *and gives it to* YANG DZ RUNG *to put back on*

BANDIT
CHIEF OF
STAFF Put it on again.

LWAN PING *realizing things have gone against him, goes forward and pleads*
Third Brother . . .

MOUNTAIN
VULTURE *shakes his sleeves at him in disgust and returns to his seat*
Humph!

LWAN PING Third Brother! *Throws himself at* YANG DZ RUNG'S *feet* Hu . . . Hu Byau, Sagely Brother!

YANG *stands impassively, ignoring him completely*

LWAN PING *slaps his own face*
I'm . . . I'm worthless scum! I ought to die! I'm trash!

YANG *to the group of bandits, shouts*
It's time! Prepare to celebrate Third Brother's birthday!

BANDITS Let's get ready to celebrate Third Brother's birthday!

BANDIT
CHIEF OF
STAFF   We can't let Third Brother's fiftieth birthday be ruined by this cur!

BANDIT
CHIEF
ADJUTANT   If we don't shoot down this evil star, it will mean bad luck for the whole mountain!

BANDITS   Yes! He must be killed! Kill him! Kill him!

LWAN PING   Elder Brothers, Hu Byau, Sagely Brother, Elder Brothers . . . Third Brother . . . Third Brother!

LWAN PING *kneels down in front of Mountain Vulture*

MOUNTAIN
VULTURE   *laughing ominously*
Ha! Ha! Ha! Ha!

LWAN PING   Save me, Third Brother!

MOUNTAIN VULTURE *waves him away*

INVINCIBLES   Kill him!

LWAN PING   Third Brother, please spare me!

BANDIT
CHIEF
ADJUTANT   Take him away!

YANG   Give him to me!

LWAN PING   Ninth Brother!

YANG DZ RUNG *grabs* LWAN PING, *who is paralyzed with fear*

YANG   *Sings*
For years wreaking evil while riding high,

Your blood debts have mounted up to the sky.
I sentence you to death in the name of the Nation.
The People shall have revenge when you die.

YANG *grabs hold of Lwan Ping's clothes and pulls him offstage.*
Shots are heard. Yang comes back onstage

YANG   Third Brother, everything's been taken care of. Now it's time to
            wish you long life.

MOUNTAIN
VULTURE   Old Ninth, you're the Officer of the Day. Whatever you say,
            goes.

YANG   Brothers!

INVINCIBLES Here!

YANG   Light the lanterns in the Hall, burn pine torches outside! Let's
            wish Third Brother a Happy Birthday!

Enter BANDIT CAPTAIN

BANDIT
CAPTAIN   Yes, it's time for the celebration to begin.

INVINCIBLES Happy Birthday, Third Brother!

All the bandits wish MOUNTAIN VULTURE *a long life*

YANG   *jumps up on a tree stump*
            Brothers! Tonight's a night for hearty eating and fierce drinking!
            No stopping until we're all drunk!

BANDITS   Yes! Yes! No stopping until we're all drunk!

YANG   Third Brother, please take the seat of honor.

MOUNTAIN
VULTURE   Uh, Brothers, please go first!

YANG Today we celebrate your fiftieth birthday. Please be seated first!

INVINCIBLES Right! Right! Third Brother, sit down first!

MOUNTAIN
   VULTURE All right, all right. Come on, everyone! *Elated* Ho, ho, ho, ho!

> *The bandits enter the cave and take their seats. Enter* BANDIT
> CAPTAIN

YANG *gets off the stump*
Captain!

BANDIT
CAPTAIN Here!

YANG Dismiss the brothers on guard. Have them come in and drink a
few cups!

BANDIT
CAPTAIN Yes sir! *Exits*

> *The bandits are heard from the cave playing drinking games and
> generally carousing.* YANG *jumps up on the stump again and
> looks around*

YANG *sings*
New Year's Eve the fortress mountain
Is strung with lanterns all ablaze.
The fiery signal has been given –
The Hundred Chickens Feast; a craze
Of bloated bandits reeling drunken.

I just hope the Comrades will quickly appear.
The time to exterminate the bandits is near.
My heart throbs as I think of the slack.
Why haven't the soldiers mounted the attack?

Frantic, I want to go out and investigate.
But in the midst of frenzy

One must stay calm.
I'll guard this secret tunnel
And wait.

Points to a spot below MOUNTAIN VULTURE'S *chair.* MOUNTAIN VULTURE, *the* BANDIT CHIEF OF STAFF, *and others stagger onstage drunk*

MOUNTAIN
VULTURE Old Ninth! Old Ninth! Why don't you come and take a seat? The Brothers are waiting to give you a toast!

YANG But today's your fiftieth birthday. We ought to be toasting you! Come on, fill up the bowl!

Everyone drinks. The sound of rifle shots. The bandits drop their winebowls. Enter an INVINCIBLE, *wounded*

INVINCIBLES Third Brother, the Communists have sealed off Tiger Hall with machine guns!

MOUNTAIN
VULTURE Ah! Brothers, quick! Let's get out of here!

BANDITS Run! Run! Run!

Voices from the PLA *can be heard: 'Throw down your guns or die!'*

MOUNTAIN
VULTURE Old Ninth! Hurry! We can get away through this secret tunnel!

MOUNTAIN VULTURE *pushes over the chair and makes for the tunnel but* YANG *shoves him over to one side*

YANG You won't get away!

Enter several PLA *soldiers shouting 'Throw down your guns or die!'*

MOUNTAIN
   VULTURE   *to* YANG DZ RUNG
       You're . . .

YANG I'm a member of the Chinese People's Liberation Army!

MOUNTAIN
   VULTURE Ah!

> MOUNTAIN VULTURE *tries to draw his gun but* YANG *strikes it to the ground.* MOUNTAIN VULTURE *runs off.* BANDITS *run into the mountain cave*

SHEN Old Yang!

YANG Comrades! There is a secret tunnel here. Save the villages inside and capture Mountain Vulture alive! *Runs offstage*

SHEN Comrades! Charge!

> PLA *soldiers charge offstage.* SHEN DE HWA *is fighting with an* INVINCIBLE *when the* BANDIT CHIEF OF STAFF *enters. The* BANDIT CHIEF OF STAFF *draws his pistol and fires at* SHEN, *who dodges. The bullet hits the* INVINCIBLE *instead and kills him.*
>
>   LWO CHANG JYANG *enters chasing an* INVINCIBLE. *They fight.* CHANG BAU *enters chasing a bandit. They wrestle and she overcomes him.* LWO CHANG JYANG *and* CHANG BAU *lead their prisoners offstage.*
>
>   *Enter* LI YUNG CHI, *the* MEDICAL ORDERLY, SOLDIERS, *and* MILITIAMEN. *They save those who had been kept prisoner on the mountain and lead them offstage.*
>
>   *The* BANDIT CAPTAIN *runs onstage and is shot dead by* LI YUNG CHI. *Another bandit runs onstage and is captured by him alive.*
>
>   MOUNTAIN VULTURE *enters in a panic, followed by two bandits in back.* YANG DZ RUNG *comes chasing after and kills the two bandits.* YANG DZ RUNG *and* MOUNTAIN VULTURE *struggle.*
>
>   JUNG JR CHENG *and* PLA SOLDIERS *chase the* BANDIT CHIEF ADJUTANT *and other bandits onstage. They fight.*
>
>   YANG DZ RUNG *grabs a rifle and shoots several bandits dead.*
>
>   *Enter* SHAU JYAN PWO, SHEN DE HWA, LI YUNG CHI, *the* MEDICAL ORDERLY GWO *and* MILITIAMEN.

MOUNTAIN VULTURE *and all the bandits are captured.*
CHANG BAU *tries furiously to stab* MOUNTAIN VULTURE *but is restrained by the* MEDICAL ORDERLY

SHAU *grasps* YANG DZ RUNG'S *hand, with great emotion*
Old Yang!

YANG Chief of Staff!

SHAU JYAN PWO *introduces* LI YUNG CHI *to* YANG DZ RUNG. *The two shake hands enthusiastically. All freeze in a dramatic pose*

Curtain